U.S. Armed Forces

Arsenal

A Guide to Modern
Combat Hardware

Samuel A. Southworth

DA CAPO PRESS
A Member of the Perseus Books Group

Copyright © 2004 by Da Capo Press

Cataloging-in-Publication data for this book is available from the
Library of Congress.

ISBN 0-306-81318-1

Da Capo Press books are available at special discounts for bulk pur-
chases in the U.S. by corporations, institutions, and other organiza-
tions. For more information, please contact the Special Markets
Department at the Perseus Books Group, 11 Cambridge Center,
Cambridge, MA 02142, or call (800) 255-1514, (617) 252-5298, or e-mail
special.markets@perseusbooks.com.

First Da Capo Press edition, 2004.

Published by Da Capo Press
A Member of the Perseus Books Group
http://www.dacapopress.com

1 2 3 4 5 6 7 8 9—07 06 05 04

Printed and Bound in the United States of America.

Contents

Preface

WEAPONS ARE A fascinating topic in military history, and provide for some of the greatest insights—and most heated debates—in military strategy discussions. Wrapped up in the metal, wood, and plastic of weapons is an entire narrative of mankind's (women included—Joan of Arc didn't fight with a feather duster, after all) incredible ingenuity for defending and conquering. And given their intimate connection to survival, it's pretty easy to let weapons take on a life of their own. Weapons can seem as if they are the answer to all of our problems (they aren't), or the cause of all of our problems (this is a trace off the mark as well). But at the end of the day it is not the weapons, it is we—or our chosen warriors—who take up those weapons and decide when, in the course of defending or conquering, civilized discourse with an opponent has reached an end, and we will seek to force a conclusion by whackin' the other guy upside the head. The study of weaponry leads one to wade through the charnal houses of every historical conflict from Sargon I of Sumeria to Saddam Hussein. (In one of those elliptical orbits that delight historians, they probably claimed the same patch of desert at one time or another.) Weapons are, indeed, fascinating, because they are the linchpins of conflict resolution, and the history of the world has so far been mostly the history of conflict.

And therein lies one of the underpinnings of this book. I have endeavored not only to look at the entire range of the modern United States military arsenal, from pistols to laser cannons, but also put each piece of gear into historical context. In doing this, I hope to excite a wider audience—the mythical "average intelligent reader." And I've added a lot of my own thoughts to the mix, as well. There's plenty of stuff in here that isn't "military" in the strictest sense, but that's all right, neither am I.

A number of years back there was a delightful book called *The Thinking Man's Guide to Baseball*, which not only introduced thoughtful readers to the dark soul of Ty Cobb, but also discussed the physics of hitting and the psychology of the squeeze play. To me, a young person enamored of military history who found himself among Red Sox fans (and fine people they are, too), this book seemed like a godsend. It enlivened and enlightened any number of lazy summer evenings spent listening on an AM radio to the Sox at Fenway. Warfare is not a game, but the approach of that book made a strong impression on me, and seemed as if it gave due credit to the reader's intelligence and thirst for "context." It is my hope that my lifelong fascination with weapons—and where they came from—has turned into a book that can be read by almost anyone, with equal parts information, context, and entertainment.

I have laid the book out so that we begin with small arms and proceed through tanks and vehicles to ships, helicopters, and jets, and then to high-tech and the future—each chapter building and expanding on the last. I hope that this style and structure will allow readers to get a general overview of what our country is using right now, and what we may use in wars to come. What I wished to avoid was an off-putting and boring list of specifications and jargon, although the temptation to babble in "Pentagonese" and "defense-industry speak" was overwhelming at times. Here you will not find dense thickets of acronyms and boring spec sheets. Though at times, I simply couldn't help myself, thinking that it was important to give an "exact" engine type, or length of a ship, or wingspan of a jet. But I always do it with a wink, and you can train your eye to blip over those parts. (If you must have it, there are plenty of other sources of this bizarre form of nearly incomprehensible communication available to you in the wide world of weapon talk, usually found in publications that cater to the selling and buying of Armageddon.)

While it may seem as if I had access to a staggering amount of information, and some of it perhaps classified, I can assure you that everything I've written about is out there to be found by anyone with a library card and access to Google. I've given nothing away to any current or potential enemy. But if our enemies do read this book and decide they still want a piece of us, I'd advise them not to try it. They'll be sorry.

A few notes on my background seem germane at the start. I am not a military man, although I registered for the draft in 1980. Everything I know comes from books and discussions with experts, so very little here is firsthand knowledge. I am a civilian writing for civilians. If you're a cranky tank driver who has thrown more treads than I've had hot breakfasts don't bother getting all heated up when you read this book. Come on, tank drivers and the like, give me a break. If you've had the training and used all this stuff, write your own book. I have had none of the training and have never fired a cruise missile. What I'm up to is a good-faith attempt to inform the public about what is in our modern arsenal, and put all of these weapons systems into a larger frame of reference.

I have the deepest respect for all of our soldiers who have fought in combat, from the ragtag and bobtail militia that stood on Lexington Green in April of 1775, right on up to the young men and women engaged in the very difficult occupation of Iraq. I'm fortunate in that my father was an officer in the United States Naval Reserve and served in combat through the entirety of World War II—from Africa and Sicily to Borneo and Leyte Gulf. As a result, I've heard a lot of Navy talk over the years—and some of it is even printable. But my father was also attached to the 1st Marine Raider Battalion, and the U.S. Army as naval liaison officer under General Lucian Truscott, and Dad always spoke very highly of both the Marines and the Army. My uncle, Philip Hobson Jr., was a Marine who was killed in Korea at age twenty in 1952, and his letters and the stories about him have given me some slight understanding of the cost of war on a very personal level. My sister and her husband were both sergeants in the USAF, and I've dealt with Coasties (U.S. Coast Guard) over the years at sea. There aren't any of the branches of service that I don't appreciate and respect. I learned their histories, and pondered their weapons, and what you have before you is the result of decades of reading and thinking about "arms and the man."

Fortunately, there were also many writers I encountered early on in life who helped me become the author of this present volume. I would be a cad not to mention the late Ian Hogg, whose overwhelming knowledge was matched by his sly sense of humor and his legendary generosity in helping researchers at the drop of a firing pin. Astute readers will hear echoes of Hogg's style, and while we never met, something tells me we would have had a great deal to talk about. I also read Bill Jordan's excellent book *No Second Place Winner* very early on in my life. His common sense and dry Texas-drawling goofiness have never left me. Here was a guy you wanted on your side in a shootin' affair. He was also, by all accounts, a man who knew when not to shoot—and I respect that just as much as his ability to wade into dark and desperate places and emerge as the victor.

My prejudices and private enthusiasms are all my own, if informed by experts. I like the M1911 Colt .45 and the 5-inch naval gun because my father said they were both fine weapons. I'm a pretty good shot against clay pigeons and cans on a fence, and my mother owns—and lends me—a Winchester Model 21 side-by-side 20-gauge shotgun. (If you keep your eyes open you'll see the Model 21 pop-up in this book like a startled grouse here and there. What's it doing in a book on military weaponry? Well, it's just the finest American shotgun ever made, and as such takes its place beside the Colt Peacemaker and M1911 as a benchmark of what our industry can produce.) I am also very fond of thinking about things in a pretty freewheeling way, and if that makes this book unsuitable for ponderous debates at the Pentagon, well, so be it. Because, while my sympathies are always with the men and women in the field, I am pretty suspicious of most of our leadership—it is they, after all, whose talents decide when and where the shooting will start, even if they show a great deal less talent for when the shooting will stop. The old saw was "War is too important to be left to the generals." I would update this old wisdom by reminding all civilians that we would do well not to let weapon manufacturers dictate how we should live and how we should die. They're doing both right now—and at a hefty profit. I have always looked askance at the defense industry; President Eisenhower's last speech on the dangers of the military-industrial complex always glowed in my thoughts like a night-vision device. If Ike thought that was the most important thing to leave us with, I am inclined to keep it in mind.

But let's face it, there's no way to discuss weapons without also talking about how and when to use them, when to simply show them or cock them, or even when not to use them. There can be no doubt that gun violence is a plague upon our country—and the incidents that get the most press are just the tip of the iceberg. And yet, America throughout its entire history has had a very close relationship with guns. There is no debate over the fact that we needed them and weren't shy about using them, from Plymouth and Jamestown all the way to Baghdad and the Hindu Kush. It isn't an empty phrase to state that our freedom and way of life were fought for and secured with guns. As a shooter and enthusiast of any weapon that is well made and operates like a bank vault door (think "Model 21"), I strongly believe that we need to have a better discussion about the role of guns in our society—one that is far removed from the position of the two extremes.

So as you can see, this isn't an ordinary book on guns and tanks and all sorts of weaponry. It's the carefully considered opinions of one man about today's weapons and their context, written by a military historian who is a great fan of diplomacy, and a shooter (and decent fencer). I prefer settling things without guns and swords, but I like keeping guns and swords near at hand. This is a complex world, and demands a complicated frame of reference to thrash through all of life's thickets and blow downs. We can't just use C4 and flamethrowers on everything—or everyone—we don't understand. Instead, we have to use the gray mass inside our heads to know how and when to use weapons—and knowing their history and implications helps.

CHAPTER 1

Shootin' Irons: Pistols and Small Arms

IN A WORLD of weapons of mass destruction, chemical, nuclear, and biological nightmares, fast-moving jets and helicopters, cruise missiles and more-or-less effective missile defense systems, aircraft carriers and submarines, it's easy to forget that nobody has yet come up with a better way to make the enemy surrender than to put well-trained soldiers in that enemy's capital city with rifles in their hands. Even then, as recent events have shown, there may be a way to go before you can declare a complete victory, but small arms will always play a crucial role in any armed conflict despite what firestorms of other technology are released along the way. Various ineffective cruise missile strikes of the 1990s back up this point, as does the study of the effect of strategic bombing in both Germany during the 1940s and Vietnam in the 1960s. In neither case was bombing alone the decisive factor for victory. Even the massive artillery barrages of

1

World War I often left the German barbed wire intact, and the wily enemy simply emerged from their underground bunkers to man the machine guns as the British and French attacks staggered through No Man's Land.

The rise of small arms to dominance was a slow process, partly because so much of their lethality was squandered by poor manufacturing and inefficient combustion of the propellant black powder. Due to the dodgy nature of early muskets and the difficulties of training often ignorant soldiers in their use, companies of men made do with simply leveling their rifles in the general direction of the enemy and trying to fire them at the same time, hoping that this rain of shot would make up for any lack of accuracy. And often it did. But by the time of the American Civil War, improvements in gunnery at all levels led to the ability to extend both the range and accuracy of everything from rifles to cannons, and when the tactics of the time failed to keep pace, the result was a slaughter that horrified such diverse observers as Walt Whitman and various European military visitors. Coupled with fanatic bravery and a certain native American stubbornness, some regiments simply melted away during their valiant attacks under the withering fire of minie balls and cannister.

Despite the rapid pace of firearms development, such innovations as the Henry repeating rifle and the Gatling gun were not embraced enthusiastically by the commanders of America's military. The feeling among the brass hats seemed to be that the average soldier would get overly excited during life-and-death encounters and just blast out all his rounds until he had exhausted his supply, and from a civilian point of view this "spray and pray" approach is pretty appealing for dealing with the forces of darkness. But the limitations that were imposed on our troops by this Luddite thinking could be tragic when coupled with impetuous leadership and a savvy foe.

Thus we have Colonel Custer's 7th Cavalry using single-shot rifles against repeating Winchesters during their dust-up with the indigenous peoples along the Little Big Horn in 1876, and while the after-action reports were made entirely by other units who found the bodies, we can assume that the lack of firepower made for a most trying day in Montana for the 7th. When the only surviving member of your command is a horse named "Comanche," you know you've been outgunned. The outcome was a little different in 2003 during the Iraq War, when at one point a Green Beret A Team of twelve men took on an Iraqi division and actually pushed them back—but of course it helps being able to call in the entire flight wing of an aircraft carrier, as well as carrying the M4 carbine with an M203 40mm grenade launcher mounted beneath the rifle barrel. No military historian could watch the footage from Afghanistan in 2001 of Special Forces on horseback without conjuring up various time-travel scenarios: "With just a couple of M4/M203s in Jeb Stuart's command…"

The bolt-action 1903 Springfield rifle in .30-caliber was an excellent weapon that saw service as our main long arm in World War I right through to Vietnam, where a few old-school snipers insisted that nothing new shot quite like it. And the M1 Garand, which was adopted by the U.S. Army in 1932, was the first semi-automatic rifle to be issued service-wide anywhere in the world. But even that fine weapon, listed (along with the Jeep and the atomic bomb) as one of the decisive factors in winning the war, had just an eight-shot clip that made a distinctive "ping!" when it ejected the clip upon firing the last shot, a sound that the Germans and Japanese learned to listen for carefully, because it meant a pause in the firing while the American GI stuffed another clip in the top of his Garand.

The Browning Automatic Rifle (BAR) was another of John Browning's little ideas (he being one of the most prolific and

The venerable Garand rifle, as used by the Silent Drill Team of the USMC. This WWII-era semi-automatic rifle was the one to beat for years, hindered only by its eight-shot clip and the distinctive "ping!" it makes when it ejects. Better hope some crusty gunnery sergeant doesn't show up and find these rifles on the ground.

influential gun designers of all time, of everything from pistols to heavy machine guns) that reflected the French and British experience in the muddy hell of Flanders and Verdun. The idea was to have some weapon that would fire shots one after another pretty quickly as one walked slowly through the mud and wire

Seen here as depicted in the Korean War Memorial in Washington, D.C., the BAR was an automatic rifle designed for the WWI trenches, but it went on to serve for fifty more years in every clime. This man is shown wearing one of the cheesy ponchos that the U.S. used for many years because they were cheap and plentiful, and the quartermaster assumed they would be thrown away in combat after the rain stopped. The BAR shown has a bipod on the barrel, as well as a handle to help change barrels if overheating rears its head.

toward the opposing team, covering the progress of one's fellows armed with bolt-action rifles. And a slight variant of this did indeed become the standard squad of World War II, in that there would be a sergeant with an M1 carbine or a Thompson submachine gun, leading a group of men with M1 Garands, and they would have a BAR man along in case somebody needed a good hosing. If things got sticky close-up and personal, Sarge could haul out his Colt .45 automatic pistol, take the safety off and rack the slide to put one of those short, squat shells in the chamber; and it didn't take more than one of those to drop someone, including chaps the size of NFL linemen. The bullet didn't travel very fast, but it had the effect of a sledgehammer, and this was found to be a great comfort.

But the Garand was a little heavy and could only use its eight-shot clip (it had no single-shot capability; you used a full clip or else swung it like a club); the BAR was really heavy, restricting its use to big fellows; the Thompson was heavy and expensive to manufacture; the M1 carbine was a little light and didn't have the range of the Garand; the Colt .45 was quite heavy and hard to shoot accurately. The armed forces of the United States spent a great deal of time on marksmanship, especially the U.S. Marine Corps, and this, coupled with our nation's some-what troublingly intimate relation with firearms as the be-all and end-all of conflict resolution, produced an army that could fire very accurately and quickly when push came to shove. But you can see where we were headed: toward lighter weight and bigger magazines. Lessening the pounds meant that a weapon would be both easier to carry and easier to train with; also, as the bullets got smaller and faster, more ammunition could be carried, and combat soldiers are a little obsessed with the amount of ammo they can take with them, for obvious reasons.

The M14 rifle (meant to replace the M1 Garand) had a 20-shot clip, but it was still pretty heavy. It wasn't until the Armalite Company developed the AR-15 in 5.56mm (.223 caliber) during the late 1950s that the modern age of American infantry weapons began to blossom. While even such a redoubtable authority as Ian Hogg doubts that we will see any surprising new twists in the field of small arms, and certainly nothing as dramatic as the exceptional innovations and progress of the twentieth century,

A sniper waits inside the U.S. embassy in Kabul, his specially tweaked M-14 at the ready. His finger is off the trigger, but nearby, and he is watching the crowd outside for any sign of hostility. Note the built-up cheek piece on the stock, and the little flaps to protect the delicate optics on his scope. The M-14 was an attempt to make the M-1 Garand more like the BAR, and has a 20-shot clip which can be released by pushing forward that little metal piece just behind the magazine.

there are still new developments being announced from time to time, and even the hopelessly quaint bolt-action rifle still has a role to play, although now as a sniping weapon or as an "anti-material" rifle when bumped up to the .50-caliber range. Thus a modern squad might have soldiers with M4/M203s as the standard long arm, a SAW (Squad Automatic Weapon) of Belgian design in the BAR role, perhaps a Barrett .50 or even a Mossberg Winchester, or Benelli 12-gauge pump-action shotgun (depending on the mission, either smiting the enemy at great range or clearing a block in Baghdad), and the high-magazine capacity of the Italian-designed Berretta M92 automatic pistol as their sidearm. This rather confirms the great thinker who said: "History does not repeat itself ... but it does rhyme."

The next generation of rifle is planned to have both a .223 barrel and magazine (like the M16/M4 of today) as well as a 20mm barrel coupled with fancy sights for seeing through darkness and smoke, and the ability to accurately predict the range to a given target and make the 20mm shell explode when it is in the proper proximity, such as when firing at an enemy inside a house. The shell will know when it has gone through the window, but instead of striking the back wall or exiting through a doorway, it will blow up in the middle of the room, which should disconcert almost any opponent. The combination of a highly accurate, small-caliber, high-velocity rifle with an infantryman's own private light artillery should prove to be most effective, and do the two things required of small arms in the U.S. military: to give comfort, confidence, and lethal options to the soldier in the field by using an intelligently designed system that can be manufactured for not much over $1500 per unit, and to slay as many of the bad guys as possible before the rest surrender.

In late 2003, news came that the retirement of the M16A2 had almost arrived, as troops in Iraq reported that it was too long to use in vehicles, and too fussy about sand in its works. Some dismounted tankers looked around them and simply adopted the ubiquitous AK-47 as having better knockdown power and easier maintenance, but the next assault rifle is evidently going to get off the drawing board and into combat very quickly. So far it is called the OICW (Objective Individual Combat Weapon), and we'll see it soon.

Pistols

Americans love their pistols, and this despite the fact that it is one more thing to carry, and only the very patient and gifted can hit things the size of a man at much beyond twenty-five yards. In the sphere of military conflicts, they often are of too small a caliber to make much of a difference on the battlefield, and their short barrels don't have the chance to stabilize the bullet for long enough to make it reliably hit what is being aimed at. And yet both commanders and some troops have traditionally carried side arms, and they can be handy little beasts within the confines of a room or a jungle clearing. George Washington had a number of matched sets of finely made flintlock pistols (to go in saddle holsters), while Andrew Jackson killed at least one unfortunate fellow in a duel before he became president, and General George S. Patton was famed for his pearl-handled revolvers (being a fan of both the single-action Colt .45 and the then-new .357 magnum). And of course, even the lilliputian Derringer managed to change the course of history when a deranged southern-sympathizing actor took one to a theater in Washington one night in April of 1865.

American pistols have often been the standard by which the rest of the world has judged their own side arms. The single-action Colt .45 and the Remington revolver were astonishing weapons for their day, in that six shots could be fired as fast as your thumb could ear back the hammer to revolve the cylinder and bring up the next round, and this in an age when loading a rifle often still meant stuffing the ball and shot down the spout with a ramrod. Various desperados could even "fan" the hammer, using their free hand to work the mechanism very quickly when a lot of lead seemed better than just one. But even when double-action revolvers came into being (where the hammer did

Some Special Forces have retained the old Colt .45, such as these Marines shown firing the MEU. Note the lanyard and flashlight, although some Special Forces (and law enforcement) hold the light to one side, where an answering bullet might find just empty air. The Colt .45 retains its reputation as a fast way to knock bad people down—as well as scaring the user if he doesn't have a great deal of training.

not have to be involved with the rotation and firing—just pull the trigger), the U.S. military resisted the notion for a long time. Being cantankerous by nature, American soldiers of the mid-to-late 1800s often equipped themselves as they thought best, trusting that the official dweebs of the Quartermaster Corps were unlikely to get too close to any actual fighting, and this resulted in such oddities (among the Confederates) as the LeMatt revolver, which was a French design that had an eight-shot cylinder with a sawed-off single-shot, 12-gauge in the middle—quite the formidable weapon! Jeb Stuart carried two; obviously not a man with whom to trifle.

But it wasn't until the adoption of the M1911 Colt .45

Automatic that an American pistol was of such fine and simple design that it would serve its country for the better part of a century. The Colt operates by the gas of each shot working a slide on top of the pistol that ejects the spent cartridge case and re-cocks the pistol as a spring forces the next round into the chamber. It has a clip of seven fat little bullets that slips into the butt of the gun; and if you were really reckless you could carry another in the chamber and have the weapon cocked with the safety on— there is hardly anybody who will tell you that this is a good idea unless you have eight hostile folks standing about one-hundred yards away and giving every indication that they have not only seen you, but intend you some close-up and personal bodily harm in the next sixty seconds.

Previously the standard side arm of the early twentieth century had been either a Colt or Smith & Wesson double-action revolver in either .38 or .45, and there are plenty of shooters who will tell you that there was nothing wrong with these fine guns except their limitation of six shots in a standard cylinder, or five shots if you were a "nervous Nelly" and left one chamber empty for the hammer to rest safely upon. Dropped guns do have a tendency to go off with mostly embarrassing and sometimes fatal results, after all. Revolvers are also a little slow to reload, in that you have to swing out the cylinder, empty the used shell casings, and fit another six into where the empties came out, and then close the cylinder before resuming your attempt to influence history around you at short range. With the Colt .45 Automatic (which is not really automatic in the sense of a modern machine gun, but more strictly a semi-automatic in that one squeeze of the trigger produces one loud noise), when the clip is empty the slide cleverly stays to the rear with the action open. You then deftly press a small button on the left side of the grip with your thumb causing the spent clip to fall out, and smack in another clip. Then

A line of Marines firing their 9mm service automatics. Note the Gargoyle sunglasses, Kevlar vests, and computer-generated camouflage that the USMC has pioneered. It is a series of tiny squares in a random pattern. These men are using the two-handed stance that has become the standard for firing pistols, and while it does make them steadier, it doesn't increase their range or lethality in combat. The first man in line is also wearing Nomex fire retardant gloves such as pilots use.

you release the slide and there you are: the most dangerous person with a pistol in your part of the world.

Firing the Colt Automatic is a very satisfying experience, in that there is all the noise and recoil that anyone could hope for in such a small package (which actually isn't that small). But the fact that it scares the bejesus out of the person firing it (along with pretty unfailingly discouraging the person hit by the bullet from ever doing anything to anger you again) is also a major

drawback. All but the most insensitive users will develop a flinch in anticipation of the shock to come when that trigger is pulled, and when this happens your rounds will go far and wide, pretty much everywhere except where you wish them to go. The British had this experience in World War I with their Webley revolvers, and as a result shifted to the Enfield .38 revolver for their next tussle with the gang from Berlin, while the Germans had the fine (if complicated) Luger and then the Walther P-38, both of 9mm.

The Japanese had terrible little pistols that weren't made very well and served mostly to anger the Marines that they were fired at during cave and jungle go-rounds.

In the late 1980s the U.S. military ran one of the most thorough and thoughtful competitions for a replacement for the old Colt, and the winner was a 9mm high-capacity automatic made by the Berretta Company of Italy, famed gunmakers who inhabit a sleepy hill town where they make fantastic pistols, shotguns, and submachine guns. The Model 92F is now made under license in the United States, and the first order was for more than 300,000 of them, underlining the confidence of the testing team that they had found the right pistol. It weighs a little over two pounds, has an almost five-inch barrel, and the magazine carries fifteen 9mm bullets in a double row that feeds one at a time upward as needed. There is an ambidexterous safety as well as two other ways to block the firing pin, and the grip and trigger guard were modified to make two-handed shooting easier.

The Berretta has a few other little improvements over the old Colt, such as the doubling of the magazine capacity, and the lesser shock of the 9mm rounds when they go off. It is a pleasant and tidy package and a joy to shoot, and nobody ever said any of those things about the Colt. You can also carry it with a full magazine, the chamber empty and the safety on, and when you get nervous and expect that there will be a problem in the near future, you simply take the safety off and pull the trigger. The first pull is a little longer than subsequent ones, because it not only fires the pistol, but also feeds that first round into the chamber without the need to work the slide or cock the hammer—just slick and easy, the way soldiers like their gear to be designed.

The Berretta has a lanyard ring in case you're kind of butter-fingered in the field, and a nice holster that holds another magazine in case fifteen shots hasn't settled your contretemps.

This new holster can be worn low and strapped to the leg like an Old West gunslinger, and there are a number of other ways to carry it, such as a cross-draw holster and one that attaches to your Kevlar vest almost like a shoulder holster, these latter two methods being preferred in cases where you're mostly inside a vehicle like the Bradley or flying a helicopter.

The troops report that any lingering wistfulness about the passing of the old Colt .45 is more than made up for by the large number of bullets and the ease of operation of the Model 92F Beretta. It should be pointed out, though, that as with any automatic, if you get a bad round or a jam you still need two hands to work the slide and bring up what you hope will be a better shell. This is where the old revolvers had an edge—in the case of a misfire, you simply worked the trigger again and the next shell was right there, and usually that one worked. Some MPs still carry revolvers, as do a few old-school police officers in the U.S. who do not anticipate lengthy firefights.

Some elite units have gone a little farther afield and secured the SIG P-229 in .40 caliber, or the Heckler & Koch Mark 23 Mod O in .45, which is an amazing pistol system that can be outfitted with laser sights and a suppressor that lowers the sound of firing by twenty-five decibels. Both of these companies are well known for making very fine (and expensive) pistols that are absolutely first-class, and it is no wonder that some soldiers with finicky jobs such as hostage rescue would seek out the best there is to be had in the world.

While there is still some chagrin that Ruger and Colt did not manage to win the competition and keep the official American military pistol one of American manufacture, at the end of the day it's all about getting the job done, and if an Italian pistol is the best choice for the moment, then so be it. Perhaps the native companies will use this setback to hone their designs and produce the next generation of side arms, because, after all, there will always be a place in armed conflict for that little something extra that only a good pistol can provide.

Assault Rifles

Back when trench warfare was the most pressing concern of the U.S. military, there was a funny little device called the Pederson that could actually change a bolt-action '03 Springfield into a very rough and ready assault rifle. It did not work very well, and was shelved with the advent of the BAR and later, the M1 Garand. If there had been a spring offensive of 1919, perhaps this attempt to give every man a machine gun-like rifle would have come to fruition. The Garand was replaced after Korea by the M14 rifle with a 20-shot clip, and this in turn gave way, at the very start of the Vietnam War, to the M16 family of weapons. These grew out of the fertile mind of armaments genius Eugene Stoner, who designed the AR10 rifle in the late 1950s. The M16 didn't just sweep the world before it, though; due to a change in the propellant powder in the Remington .223 cartridge and the myth that it was a "maintenance-free rifle" (as if!), the new long arm got a bad reputation for stoppages that were annoying on the firing range and fatal in combat. But as a result of working through these little details, which mostly entailed the long suffering sergeants of America making sure that every soldier cleaned their weapon every day (as they have been doing since the 1700s), the M16 soon proved to be a world beater, and versions of it are still out there firing away in every climate and time zone.

At six pounds it is about two-thirds of the weight of a Garand, and the early models were thirty-nine inches long, which made for a handy package in the jungle. Best of all it could

A USMC instructor teaching a Latvian soldier to shoot an M-16, and staring directly at the problem: the shooter's left hand has an improper grip on the front stock. It should be cradled in the palm to aid in accuracy by providing a more stable shooting platform. Next line after this picture was taken? "You might want to slide your hand under that front stock a little more, buddy, and tilt yer helmet back a little."

take either twenty- or thirty-round clips. The Green Berets, for instance, in SOG during their clandestine patrols over the border into Cambodia and Laos, would typically carry twenty of these clips, as well as carrying a shortened version of the M16 (called the Colt Commando, or less euphoniously, the XM177E2) that would come in time to replace it. The M16A2 was the improved

Gun safety applies at all times. Here a corporal pulls back the bolt of his M-4 carbine to check that the breach is empty. Notice he has taken the clip out and the rifle is pointed safely upward. The M-4 was a Special Forces system that came to be adopted by the military at large due to its handy size.

version that was released in 1983, but before too long an interesting phenomenon came about: a Special Forces idea (the shortened M16) actually became the standard rifle of the U.S. military. The new M4 is a very tidy assault rifle verging on a submachine gun, with a collapsible stock and a range of additions that can be grafted onto it, such as modern "see through smoke and dark" sights, and the M203 40mm grenade launcher, and even a shotgun barrel that can fit under the rifle barrel. It is accurate out to about three hundred meters, although it cannot be easily carried in tight spaces such as the inside of a Bradley Fighting Vehicle.

There is a bayonet for the M4, but you better not use it if you don't want everybody else to laugh at you. Bayonets in the field are mostly used for food preparation and minor medical procedures, and hardly anyone misses the idiocy of bayonet practice except for the occasional mad major. Still, a few historians will remember old Josh Chamberlain and the proud 20th Maine turning the tide of battle on the second day of Gettysburg with guts and steel. And there was the Korean War vet who wrote about being stationed with Turkish UN troops who were surrounded by thousands of Chinese while trapped on a hilltop. He was both chilled and exhilarated to hear the fixing of the Turks' bayonets and their gleeful laughter, because it seemed they were looking forward to getting away from mere sissy bullets and thrashing it out with cold steel. And that hilltop never did get taken by the Chinese.

Consider what the rest of the world is using for rifles: bullpup designs for the British and French (where the magazine is behind the trigger enabling a long barrel to exist in a short length) and the venerable Kalashnikov in all its incarnations for (seemingly) everybody else. Thanks, Russia! These AKs are fine and tough weapons that are as close to maintenance free as any weapon will ever get, and have proven themselves around the world as hardy and deadly arms for the masses. Even so, the M4 is a superbly made assault rifle that throws its .223 bullet out at a phenomenal 3,200 feet per second, and as a result, a bullet almost the same size as the old .22 Long Rifle cartridge, beloved of plinkers for a century, has the ability to hit as hard as a battle ax,

The next American rifle? A Marine pilot checks out the ubiquitous AK-47. This legendary rifle is famously sturdy, accurate and hard-hitting, and requires very little maintenance in the field. Why can't we build 'em like that?

and often with about the same result. The U.S. military has come a long way from the Pederson device.

Shotguns

Shotguns in combat? You bet! And depending on how you understand the rules of modern warfare (as well as the simple and perhaps fallacious notion that there are any rules), shotguns remain a great way to use a powerful firearm with proven stopping ability that has a fairly short range (not always a bad thing, such as when fighting around your friends or civilians in houses or streets or jungles). There is also the psychological impact of a scattergun, which makes it ideal for patrolling fractious districts in unhappy lands. Hardly any bad people are so rowdy as to want to tangle with the big black hole at the end of a shotgun's muzzle, or to keep doing what you wish them to stop doing when that unmistakable sound of the slide being worked punctuates your request for compliance, as law enforcement has long known.

Mossbergs, Benellis, Winchesters in 12-gauge are the preferred variety of weapon when something or somebody just needs to be blasted and marksmanship isn't that big a deal, and nobody in their right mind would go into combat with anything other than a pump action. Side-by-sides and over-and-unders are sporty, and autoloaders are deadly with ducks and clay pigeons, but the pump gets the job done best during crunch time because there is hardly any way to stop it from functioning short of breaking it over someone's skull. Bad shell? Jammed ejection? Just keep working the pump and all will be well for you, and unwell for your enemy. The Winchester 1897 was the first pump gun to make its way into combat, and quickly got the reputation of a "trench broom" because of its robust action and quick shooting. With the old '97 you could actually just hold the trigger down and work the pump as fast as you liked, with a satisfying explosion every time the gun was cocked. This "hosing" ability was highly prized among the more bloody-minded users. Modern-day shotguns are built with a few more safety features than in the good old days, but they still can spray buckshot or sabot rounds or slugs (which are big bullets) very quickly and effectively, and if you're going into a tight place (physically and emotionally) a shotgun isn't a bad thing to push ahead of you, as SWAT teams have learned through hard experience.

Bolt-Action Rifles

What possible role could the old bolt-action have on the modern battlefield? Didn't they go out with trench knives and satchel charges? Actually, all three are still with us, and will be as long as imaginative options are important to the pursuit of martial aims. But this isn't your great-grandfather's Springfield Ought Three. Modern bolt-action rifles are mostly of two types: those used by snipers, and the new breed of "anti-material" weapons such as the Barrett Fifty, which is an astoundingly long-range rifle of .50 caliber that can defeat trucks and even Scud missiles on their launchers, to say nothing of vaporizing any poor person it hits. Originally a semi-automatic, the Barrett has morphed into a bullpup-configured bolt-action, and is as lethal as a missile against many targets. It's a gigantic bullet that arrives without any noise and heralds the end of anything it hits.

The standard modern-day sniping system for everyday use when the Barrett seems like overkill (which is almost always) is the M24, which is a Remington rifle toned down from its civilian roots as a hunter's favorite. It fires a .300-magnum round quite a long way out, almost three quarters of a mile, and with its five-round magazine you'll have four more chances if this is your first mission and you're a bit jittery. Just work that bolt smartly! Get a good 8- or 10-power scope on top and you have a pretty lethal and modern combination, although it has been pointed out that even old Italian rifles can change the course of history.

Snipers go through a lot of training to enable them to operate as sneaky two-man teams, a shooter and a spotter.

Covering one hundred yards in an afternoon isn't unusual for them, creeping on their bellies like reptiles while dressed as a shrub, because it may take such extraordinary fieldcraft skills to get to where the best shot can be taken. Snipers are viewed with great anger by the enemy, and often suspicion by their own side because of the stealthy nature of their calling. Sniping seems to fall in and out of favor as the years and wars roll along, but it is always a valid way to strike precise targets in a definitive way. Those targets would definitely include (as you're looking through your scope) the younger guy carrying the radio on his back and the older guy talking into the handset. These two gents are likely the communications and command of the enemy you are observing, and without them the other side may well fall apart unless they have really good NCOs (as the British and Americans are known to have).

Snipers love their work, and are known for lengthy and arcane discussions concerning different powder loads and various rifles and scopes that make little sense to outsiders. When snipers go bad, as in Dallas and Houston and in the DC area within recent memory, they demonstrate that not only are they highly effective at changing the world with a very few shots, but also that amazing and deadly actions are not all that hard for the committed (or the committable). As a deadly skill with one foot in darkness, sniping will remain a valuable talent given (thankfully) to only a few.

CHAPTER 2

Belt and Box: Machine Guns

IF YOU WERE putting together a greatest hits soundtrack of warfare, you'd probably have some rumbling tanks and artillery noises; some helicopter clatter and a jet zoom or two; perhaps a sergeant yelling orders over the cacophony; but you would most certainly have somewhere in there the "rat-a-tat-tat" of the familiar machine gun. Nothing says "I bear you ill will" quite as definitively as those rattling bursts.

The machine gun as we know it is simple in its appeal to those tasked with smiting a foe: if one person shooting at the enemy is a good idea, then a regiment shooting at the enemy is a better one, and one man shooting the equivalent of a regiment's worth of hot lead down range has got to be the best option of all. Given an infinite amount of ammunition and the suspension of friction and heat, the idea of a steady stream of bullets flung out at the opponent by merely squeezing a trigger or depressing a lever with your thumb is simple in conception and desirability, but as with so many things, the actuality of the development and mechanism of the machine gun took quite a while to sort itself out.

There had been ancient siege machines that could be made to fling a quantity of arrows in the right general direction, but while this certainly discommoded those unlucky enough to be struck by them, it seems to have been about as effective as throwing rocks. It wasn't until Mr. James Puckle came forth with his strange gun in 1717 that we get something we can almost recognize as a machine gun. It was rather like a revolver (and indeed there has been speculation that a man named Sam Colt had been exposed to this concept at some point) in that it had a cylinder turned by a crank that fired one chamber at a time through a single barrel, utilizing the then-standard flintlock ignition system, which was basically a sharp piece of flint held in a vice that could be made to strike a metal pan and produce a spark that would then jump into the barrel and ignite the main charge. As with all flintlocks, "bad hair days" with high humidity meant the postponement of hostilities or the reversion to the tried and true axe, sword, and spear.

But the British authorities were underwhelmed by Mr. Puckle's gun, although they did purchase one. Puckle kept pushing his concept, firing sixty-three shots in seven minutes in 1722, which ain't bad for the fussy muzzle-loading era, and he even offered regular round balls for use against Christians and a separate cylinder with square holes for use against Infidels. While ballistics at the time was considered a mystical subject, the shape of the bullet has in truth only slight bearing on its lethality, but Puckle also seemed to intimate in his promotional materials that the gun was good for shooting Catholics as well, and perhaps this accounts for the one example held in the Tower of London—one never knew when the Irish would arise and have to be pacified again! As a result of official indifference, one of the great cries of military history was never to be heard on the field of conflict: "Deploy the Puckle!"

Mankind's quest for ever-increasing mayhem is hard to thwart, however, and a stream of oddities poured from the fertile minds of inventors, perhaps in a true patriotic fervor, or just as the result of domestic squabbles. There was the Perkins Steam Gun, which perhaps could derive its steam from the ship or train it was bolted upon, and Agar's "Coffee Mill," with its self-contained cartridges, and the Billinghurst-Requa battery gun with about twenty-five barrels laid out side by side. The French had the Mitrailleuse, their own 25-barrel wonder that attracted the attention of Napoleon III, who secretly (he thought) bought 156 of them for what he thought would be the final solution to his German problem. Unfortunately, a lack of range and a misunderstanding of how to use machine guns meant that not only were they shot off the field by artillery in the Franco-Prussian War of 1870, but that there would be eighty more years of backing and forthing along the Alsace. Could a more intelligent understanding of machine guns have prevented both subsequent world wars? We'll never know.

We will encounter this misunderstanding of the weapon again as the story unfolds. Are machine guns the province of the artillery, to be mounted on heavy carriages or fixed in place, or should they be thrown in the infantry's bag of tricks? There proved to be very few military thinkers who were equal to the task of grappling with this strange beast. It was correctly thought that the machine gun would make a wonderful defensive weapon, if it had some good cover and a clear field of fire, such as the approach to a fort or a previously cleared area to the front. This facet of their deployment hasn't changed a whit from the Civil War to Iraq.

This is the parlor version of the legendary Gatling gun, in .30 caliber. Gatlings came in all sizes, right up to one inch, which is a big rapid firing gun. The Gatling concept came back in the 1960s with the addition of electric feed and drive, making them the hands-down winners for throwing lead at a terrific pace. This picture also illustrates the debate about the use of machine guns, which in 1898 were still misunderstood. Here it is clear that they are seen as artillery—note the heavy mount. There were definitely horses and/or mules attached to this unit.

In an irony on a plane with the elevation of Alfred Nobel from dynamite tycoon to benefactor of peace, an American doctor by the name of Richard Gatling invented his eponymous weapon in 1861, just in time for the "War of Northern Aggression." But while General Benjamin "Spoons" Butler bought twelve of the early models, it wasn't until 1866 that the United States officially adopted the Gatling gun as we know it, in a .50-caliber and a one-inch model. The Gatling was a quantum leap in conception, in that it fired self-contained cartridges through a system whereby they fell into one of several barrels that were revolved by a crank, made a short circular trip to the bottom where they met the firing pin and were fired, and then continued up to where they were ejected, and the barrel was ready for the next cartridge to fall in. This also meant that each barrel had a little break in the action, and a chance to cool down a bit before the next internal explosion. This overheating of machine gun barrels is still an issue today.

But while the Gatling was a monster in its day, it was still as heavy as many light artillery pieces, and turning the crank did nothing to improve the accuracy of the weapon. But once again an American came to the rescue, in the form of Hiram Maxim and his handy machine gun. Both smaller and lighter than the Gatling (or its various competitors, the Hotchkiss and Nordenfeldt), the Maxim was the first gun that could reload and fire itself using the motive force of the last shot. After failing to interest any U.S. authorities in the deadly potential of his gun, Mr. Maxim went to England and became one of the great success stories of the late nineteenth century. While there was some suggestion for improvements, the Maxim was rightly seen as the wave of the future, and all sorts of variations were contemplated and manufactured, there was even one smallish model made in the pistol caliber of .32, which could be carried in a suitcase by traveling salesmen. For the defense of pubs, one wonders? Maxims were capable of a staggering rate of fire, and the Maxim-based Vickers gun was once fired for several days with an endless belt of cartridges.

Be that as it may, there is a photograph of Maxim with two visiting Chinese delegates in 1890 where it appears he has managed to chop down a tree that must be a good two feet around, and the obvious potential of this weapon wasn't lost on any of the great powers that adopted it in the next few years. Indeed, the Maxim in various forms was to be the backbone of the British and German machine-gun forces for a good many years, contributing to the carnage on the Western Front from 1914 to 1918, and being mounted on tripods, airplanes, boats, and zeppelins.

What is it about Americans and machine guns? While the Winchester lever-action rifle and the Colt revolver are seen as symbols of our country, our ongoing enthusiasm for full automatic fire is no less a mark of Yankee thinking. John Browning, one of the true giants of gun design (being the father of legendary pistols, rifles, shotguns, light and heavy machine guns, etc.), took Maxim's ideas and developed them further. From his teeming brain sprang the Colt M1895 "Potato Digger," the Browning Automatic Rifle (BAR), and the .30- and .50-caliber water-cooled and air-cooled machine guns that came to define American automatic weaponry. In these various weapons we can see all the mechanical ingenuity of a brilliant mind brought to bear on the continual thorny problem of how to best design and employ this proven and deadly technology.

With machine guns slowly being made lighter, and with new forms of feeding the ammunition into them, a rethinking was underway during World War I. To begin with, artillery killed almost twice as many men in that conflict as machine guns did, despite the popular conception that the machine gun was the stuttering angel of death on the Western Front. Machine guns were still limited by their weight and feed mechanisms, preventing them from being pushed forward in the attack. They excelled at defensive use, but even more when the concept was better understood. Machine-gun bullets first go up, and then slowly descend, and as such they have a limited area where they are effective, the rightly called "danger zone." This is from where the first bullet would strike the top of an enemy soldier to the point where the bullet descends to ground level. But not all bullets will proceed in this tidy way, and so there is actually a "beaten zone," in which they will group themselves. An understanding of this was slow to arrive, but one lesson of the function of machine guns is that if you have a choice you will wish to deploy them from the flank of an attacking force, giving you the elegant French expression "enfilade fire," which is simply more effective than shooting head-on at advancing infantry.

The heavy carriages and useless metal shields of the 1914 models gave way to lighter tripods, but most guns were still cooled by water, and that meant a two-gallon can attached by a hose to the barrel. This is hardly a unit that can be horsed around the field very easily, or pushed forward with an attack without a great deal of grunting and groaning.

American troops in World War I were saddled with French machine guns due to the difficulty and expense of manu-facturing our own. But one weapon, the Lewis Gun, seemed to be a glimpse of things to come. This light machine gun was air-cooled and had a circular drum magazine, enabling it to be thrust forward almost as quickly as rifles. Then the Browning Automatic Rifle was introduced, but not in time to influence the fields of France in 1918. Indeed, some of its first adoptions came from police agencies and the notorious John Dillinger, who along with Clyde Barrow sawed off much of the stock and barrel of the BAR and had an awesome weapon to show for their efforts.

The Browning-designed M1917 is the best example of the old water-cooled guns. It is a 32-pound, recoil-operated machine gun on a tripod, firing 250-round cloth belts using a pistol grip and trigger at the rear. To load it you open the top, carefully place a belt in, and then close the top and cock the handle on the side. Pull the trigger and it will merrily churn its way to the end of the

Don't you wish you could sit through this class? A sergeant shows some Korean War soldiers the parts of a .30-caliber water-cooled machine gun, pointing to the rear sight. The men seem transfixed in a zombie-like state that only military education can produce.

belt, given sufficient water to cool the barrel and assuming that nothing jams. If it does jam you have to work the handle again, and you may have to make sure the belt has been loaded correctly and that it is feeding as it ought. You can swing it freely about in case there is some part of the field that needs more attention, or you can traverse it very carefully in a controlled way with a system of fine-toothed gears. On the .50-caliber model (as on the heavy British and German machine guns) there was some-

A rare integrated machine-gun squad takes up a position they have dug themselves in a shell hole. When the shooter starts firing, the man on the right will make sure the belt feeds cleanly into this M1919 Browning, and stand ready with the next box.

times mounted a compass to enable the firing of selected missions of more or less accuracy, and, just as with mortars, you might do well to place aiming stakes out ahead of the gun to prevent the wild-eyed expenditure of all the ammunition without actually striking any of your opponents.

The M1917 could (with some effort) be rushed forward to support an attack, and, along with the Lewis Gun and the BAR, you could put together a tidy firestorm of lead if you had someone in the battalion who understood the changing nature of warfare. The Germans in World War I seemed to catch on most quickly, with the British trailing behind, and the Americans getting a late start but using their reputations for fast-learning and decisive violence to good effect. The French were by no means confused by machine guns, but the debacle of Verdun and the mutinies of 1917 rather put a crimp in their sails.

But it was the M1919 Browning in the massive .50 caliber that came to truly epitomize what Americans (and a good many other folks) wanted in a machine gun. It was a bit heavy, but it featured air-cooling (no more of those unwieldy two-gallon containers) and could fire such a large bullet such a long way at such a good clip that there was hardly anything that could (or can to this day) stand against it. The M1919 (after some development) went on to sweep the field both literally and figuratively, and it is hard to imagine what device could come along that would replace it, so well did John Browning understand his life's work.

World War I had seen the placement of machine guns on airplanes for the first time, and this trend was rapidly expanded. The air forces of the two sides had begun as strictly reconnaissance units, but some unfriendly soul began firing a pistol and then a rifle at the opposing team, and soon every airplane had a fast-firing gun mounted either in the rear with an observer, or facing forward on top of the wing, or, after the development of the synchronizing gear, right through the propeller. This meant that to fire the gun into an enemy plane, you steered your airship so that your nose was on the foe, and pulled the trigger. The Germans used the Parabellum, while the Allies had the Lewis Gun (in the top-of-the-wing configuration) or else the trusty Vickers firing over the nose through the prop. Both the Parabellum and the Vickers are, of course, Maxim designs.

The War To End All Wars also saw the placing of machine guns in so-called "pill boxes," sited so as to have interlocking fields

The M-2 Browning goes mobile mounted on a Hummer. The shooter is exposed, but any target he finds will have a hard time scheduling their response once this baby cuts loose. Soldiers agree that mounting heavy machine guns beats the tar out of carrying them around, although it's hard to be accurate while in motion.

of fire, and these proved to be very hard to overcome without massive casualties. If you could get to the side or behind them you could attack from the blind spot, but this was often covered by another pill box, making for a frustrating morning.

During the 1920s and 1930s interest in weaponry waned except for those countries that were secretly planning on conquering the world, or among those who suspected that this was the case and sought to arm themselves ahead of time. It is fortunate that in the M2 Browning (in both .30- and .50-caliber versions) the United States had a world-beating machine gun, and once the industrial might of the New World got its act together there came an outpouring of arms such as has never been equaled, a good many of them being machine guns. The BAR still acted as the squad automatic, sometimes replaced by the Thompson sub-

Two Marines take a pretty exposed position (marked with a flag in case opponents have difficulty spotting them), but with their .50-caliber on a tripod (the barrel just visable behind the front sight of the M16A2 with M203 grenade launcher in the foreground) they should be able to engage and defeat any enemy—such as the ferry leaving the harbor.

machine gun or later the M3 "Grease Gun," but for heavy infantry work on both offense and defense, and for mounting on tanks, jeeps, halftracks, landing craft, and airplanes, the M2 Browning was the last word in hosing down the enemy. It could still get into trouble if you didn't limit it to short bursts as the barrel could heat up to a dangerous point, but for months and years and through every corner of the globe the Browning chewed the tar out of everything it was aimed at.

During World War II the armor on tanks and airplanes began to increase as a reaction to the guns they were facing, and while the .50-caliber Browning could gnaw a hole in most anything, the automatic cannon now began its rise to prominence. Originally known as the "Pom-Pom" (in 37mm, about an inch and a half) due to its distinctive firing noise and slow ammunition feed, various models had been trotted out by all sides of every conflict since the Boer War, and mostly they were just Maxims on steroids—scaled up versions of the tried and tested design. Once you press much beyond .50 caliber, there is also enough room in the cartridge for a number of specialized shells, such as proximity fuses, white phosphorus, explosive, and armor-piercing rounds. Although the Becker cannon of 1915 is reckoned to be the first actual automatic cannon, it wasn't until 1941 that such guns began to proliferate on vehicles (mostly large vehicles) and aircraft, and mostly in 20mm and 40mm. These large rounds were very effective against aircraft and trucks, and could also simply tear up exposed infantry. The United States had all flavors of these, from the single 20mm mounted on PT boats to the "quad 40"mm placed on naval vessels to give them a chance against low-flying Japanese dive-bombers and the dreaded suicide planes of the latter part of the war. As can be imagined, four 40mm rapid-firing barrels made for one hell of a hail of shot and shell. The 20mm also found a home in the nose

The familiar spade grip and massive receiver mark this as an M-2 .50-caliber mounted on a small boat. The M-2 retains its awesome capabilities as a destroyer of hostiles even in an age of 20mm and 30mm cannons. Able to fire almost a mile, it can trash trucks, troops, light tanks, aircraft, small houses and other boats in a twinkling.

of the P-38 "Lightning," the twin-tailed terror of every truck convoy and Japanese merchant ship it ran across, there also being four .50-caliber Brownings in the nose just to sweeten the deal.

Nothing new came over the horizon until the start of the Vietnam War of the 1960s, when some restless Air Cav members began trying to improve the armament of their helicopters. The M60 machine gun in 7.62mm had replaced the BAR and .30-caliber

Browning as the standard light infantry machine gun, and this design (much of it nicked from the German MG42) was also used aboard the choppers. Navy SEALs had the option to use whatever weapon they wanted and could get their hands on, and some of them cut down the stock and barrel of the M60 (shades of Dillinger!) to make a lethal and short package for patrolling the Rung Sat, as well as using the Stoner 63 System light machine gun (designed by Eugene Stoner, father of the M16). This was a 5.56mm box-fed light machine gun that was a bit temperamental, but it had a devoted following among those willing to baby it into combat.

The M60 could have its barrel changed in a hurry, and so for the first time a really practical light machine gun was in the field with U.S. forces. But "light" is more than a state of mind, and at twenty-three pounds you still would want the squad giant nicknamed "Tiny" to be delegated to tote this thing through the jungle, and there was still the problem of carrying all those belts of ammunition. Despite the macho style of draping belts of machine-gun ammo over one's chest in the best wannabe style, you can only carry about a minute's worth of ammunition this way. The old Brownings had offered a box-fed option, as did Mr. Stoner, and soon the M60 was adapted to this sensible alternative to the awkward belt.

But the restless men of the 1st Air Cavalry Division were keen to improve their ability to spray the jungle (and hopefully pesky VC) with bullets, and soon they had taken their M60s off the pintle at the side door and mounted them either externally firing forward (giving the pilots a better sense of controlling their destinies) or else suspending them (and their enthusiastic gunners) on bungy cords in the doors of Huey helicopters, thus allowing them to fire straight down if need be, or swing around to allow for the path of the jinking chopper as it descended or rose from bullet-swept jungle clearings. It was at this point in the

Mounting an M-2 .50-caliber machine gun so that it can shoot out the back of an MH-53 Pave Low helicopter is a great way to put a sting in the tail of Special Operations rotorcraft. Note the electric ammo feed and the flexibility of the mounting pintle—this shot is to starboard at a goodly angle. The drab concrete house and scrubby pine places this in Florida. One guesses that house has been assaulted many, many times.

development of the machine gun that the General Electric Corporation brought a "good thing to light" by astoundingly reviving the Gatling principle of multiple barrels, but this time with a difference which you may have guessed by pondering the company's name: the barrels were no longer driven by a crank like some hapless organ grinder who has lost his monkey and is mad about it; instead, the electrical system of the helicopter is used to feed the ammunition into the barrels and make them go around, and at an astonishing pace. What do I consider to be astonishing? Well, how about 6,000 rounds a minute? One hundred bullets a second makes for quite the whirring noise up near the chopper, and for absolute devastation on the ground below. These Miniguns (as they were known) came in 7.62mm NATO and later in 5.56mm, the same as the M16, and were so effective that they eventually came to be the preferred method of bashing folks on the ground.

Today the M60 has gone the way of all things, and has been replaced on the ground by the clever Belgian Minimi designed by

Fabrique National. Almost ten pounds lighter than the M60, it has been taken into the U.S. arsenal as the M249 machine gun, and is the new Squad Automatic Weapon (known logically as the SAW), and as such replaces all the old designs with an intelligent response to previous wants, such as the ability to use either a 100- or 200-round box magazine that is greenish see-through plastic (to check your supply, often the source of nervous concern for good reasons in combat), as well as the clever feature of being able to simply insert a 20- or 30-round standard M16 or M4 magazine in a special slot and shoot that out without any problems. This means that you are all carrying the same ammunition, riflemen and machine gunners, and your 15-pound squad weapon is a handy forty inches long, although there is a paratrooper version that is even shorter for those whose shooting takes place in caves, houses, or dense undergrowth. It is a reliable and well-tested gun that has been enthusiastically taken over by American soldiers, and is reported to be accurate and fast to fix, and you can change the barrel quickly without removing the bipod or the carrying handle (try that with your M60!).

The heavy machine gun of choice remains the M1919 design of old John Browning, and as a reliable and battle-honored veteran of numerous conflicts, it is hard to imagine something replacing it … unless it is an automatic cannon, such as the Hughes Chain Gun. This 30mm monster once again uses electrical power to feed and fire the weapon, and the result is a highly

An M249 SAW on a tripod, which improves accuracy and can be jettisoned quickly if the squad moves up. In an odd "belt and suspenders" touch, the forward bipod is also extended, but this may indicate that the shooter expects to be moving shortly.

dangerous single-barrel gun that can destroy almost anything in its path. An automatic cannon also has the charming feature of never jamming, and indeed a gunner might not notice a dud or misfire, because the electric drive simply takes the bad with the good and throws them all out the side once they have passed through the firing chamber, and can do so at that mythical rate of 5,000 to 6,000 rounds per minute. The Chain Gun is currently featured in the nose of the AH-64 Apache helicopter, and like its namesake, this bloodthirsty gun platform can massacre the unsuspecting in jig time, including taking on tanks and armored

The commander of a Stryker is shown watching as his Bushmaster 25mm Chain Gun chews the blazes out of some far-off target. He also has a light machine gun mounted just ahead of him in case he wants to join in at some point.

vehicles, and you don't even want to know what it does to trucks and tents. The Chain Gun is linked to an optical sight mounted on the helmet of the weapons officer, and where he looks is where it points from its mounting under the chin. Then just touch the trigger and the offending sight is vaporized. This is a little different from the first pilot taking a pistol shot at a startled German plane in 1914.

The A-10 "Warthog" tank killing airplane is used for close ground support, notably by the U.S. Marine Corps, and it has a 30mm Gatling gun under its unattractive nose that has proven to be just the thing when encountering truck and tank convoys on open roads in the desert, particularly when firing the controversial depleted uranium rounds that pierce armor like butter.

Another new use for the modern Gatling has been in various sea-going protective systems stemming from the Falklands War, when British ships were attacked with Exocet surface-skimming missiles. These modern systems replace the man on the rail with a 20mm, or even the quad 40, with a Gatling linked to a radar system that first detects the incoming missile and then throws a veritable storm of lead at it, hopefully causing it to explode far from one's own ship. It's a neat idea, although you'll want to turn it off when recovering your own ship's helicopter, and so far the system hasn't been tested in actual combat, the

vogue for the Exocet seemingly having vanished with the waning of the 1980s.

Some modernization of the M1919 has been attempted, such as the Fabrique National attempt to make a 15mm gun that would fall between the .50-caliber and the 20mm, but it has not been adopted by U.S. forces just yet. The Browning is just too good, and we own too many of them. There have been efforts to speed up their rate of fire by making them feed from a box on either side of the breech, and new quick-change barrels, and a nifty stabilization platform that keeps most of the recoil away from the gunner, but the Browning M2 .50-caliber seems likely to be around long after we are gone.

The M79 shoulder-fired grenade launcher was first used in Vietnam, and then replaced by the M203 40mm grenade launcher which fits untidily under the barrel of the standard M16 or the new M4; but these days you can also take the Mark 19 machine gun with you into the field, although it's rather heavy. As a result of intelligence from the Russian invasion of Afghanistan in the late 1970s, the U.S. cobbled together this machine gun that fires 40mm grenades, and can throw them out about a half mile. It is a low recoil weapon, but too heavy to be carried very far, and so best-suited for use as a defensive gun or else mounted on a truck or Hummer.

The theory of machine guns has advanced somewhat over time, although they will always have some common characteristics.

A lance corporal is seen here clearing his M203 after taking a shot with the grenade launcher. The empty ejected shell can just be made out in the lower right. To fire again he would have to insert a fresh cartridge and slide the ridged tube to the rear, before sighting and pulling the trigger located just ahead of his M-16's magazine. Note the sight for the launcher just behind the triangular front sight of the rifle.

They tend to be a bit heavy, and are prodigious users of ammunition. They can easily deafen their users, and are easily spotted in the field because of their noise and the inevitable smoke they produce upon firing. This means that your machine-gun position will attract hostile attention soon after you go into business. Machine guns lack subtlety, but make up for it in their ability to quickly pound people and things into mush. They are not the most precise guns on the planet, although the .50-caliber will send a bullet out about a mile, and one was used in Vietnam as a sniping system with some success. They can fire a range of ammunition, from straight ball (the basic big chunk o' lead) to armor-piercing (against tanks and defenses) to tracers (used to give the gunner some feedback on the direction of his shooting) to incendiary (used to light up fuel and vehicles). They have to be fed carefully, and fired carefully lest they overheat. Short bursts are the best bet, but that can be hard to remember in the heat of combat. Your position will soon make itself known to your enemy if you're hosing him down with half-inch bullets, and he will try to bring his own machine guns to bear on you, if not artillery and/or aerial attacks.

When attacking a machine gun, soldiers try to wait for the inevitable changing of ammunition boxes, or a barrel change, and then rush forward as fast as they can. Or better yet, they try

This is just what you want your light machine gunners to do: press forward and find cover to protect the rest of the platoon as they advance. Note the carrying handle and sling to provide many options for rapid transport.

to neutralize the machine gun by helicopter or artillery means. Attacking from multiple directions will cause the enemy to disperse his fire in a helpful way. Also, machine guns are sometimes placed at important positions, so the enemy may be unconsciously signaling where his headquarters or bases are located by where he has chosen to site his guns.

Machine guns in this new century will still be of great use whenever one person confronts many who mean to harm him, and as such, although the lightweight SAW and the 30mm Chain Gun are at far ends of the spectrum, the U.S. military is likely to have them in use for many years to come. But an attack can now be started with a mix of helicopter-borne automatic cannons and fixed .50-caliber machine guns to either smoke out the enemy or keep his head down, and then squads of infantry can rush forward carrying SAWs and M203s under the barrels of their M16s or M4s, and thus project more and greater firepower closer to the enemy than ever before, and it is hoped that this will lead to briefer and more decisive firefights than in the past. One hundred-twenty years after Hiram Maxim patented his quick-firing gun, it seems that we have come to understand these contraptions a little better, and that the soundtrack of future conflicts will still feature that same old "rat-a-tat-tat."

CHAPTER 3

Air Mail: Bombs, Missiles, and Rockets

WHEN THE UNITED STATES wishes to communicate displeasure with a foreign nation, there are a number of ways they can express themselves, from stiff telegrams with arch wording and dire veiled threats, all the way up to and including the dropping of enough bombs and the launching of enough missiles to darken the skies, and subsequently blacken a goodly patch of ground as well. Indeed, in the modern age it can often seem as if the mere launching of these flame-spouting, death-dealing, harbingers of doom would be sufficient to accomplish our intentions as the sole remaining super power. But as will be seen, this is a false economy which is not in truth all that economical, and we still have to put boots on the ground and our people right in the heart of darkness to further our aims in the geopolitical sphere, be that altering the landscape and changing the governments in Afghanistan and Iraq, or grappling with the future demons of the world.

There's just something about bombs, missiles, and rockets that turns one's thoughts to the world at large (due to their range and potential for overwhelming explosions). They also can give some policymakers the illusion that they can simply touch these things off, use the same match to light a Cuban cigar, and go back to domestic policy or meeting with lobbyists, secure in the notion that they have "taken decisive action on a matter of national security and global import." But very few things in the world of military history and hardware are exactly what they seem to be, and those who misunderstand the potential and use of flying bombs (whatever they may be called: ICBM, ALCM, SLCM, MIRV, MARV, CBU-55, etc.) run the risk of taking an action that is no more decisive than stamping their foot and wishing their enemy would be nicer.

Bombs

Bombs used to be the easiest weapon to understand: simply weld a tube with a nose and a tail, put explosives in the nose and perhaps fins on the tail, take it up in a plane, find the enemy headquarters, shout "Bombs Away!" while chucking the thing over the side, and then fly home secure in the knowledge that you've really messed up THAT staff meeting. The first bombs were actually bomblets and mortar shells dropped over the side of those wood and canvas airplanes of World War I, and while this was certainly unwelcome by those on the ground, the true potential for devastation by means of bombing was only revealed to a few great thinkers, like the late unlamented General Billy Mitchell. The Germans in that war did manage to float enormous zeppelins and the massive Gotha bomber plane over the English Channel, and once over what they took to be the right place, drop quite a selection of bombs on London as well as upon unoffending cows scattered across the countryside, including a large incendiary device that seems to have consisted of rope, tar, and oil—certainly messy, if not always as deadly as intended.

Jules Verne had been among those who saw this wave of the future, along with H. G. Wells, but the reaction of those being bombed was most interesting. Instead of emerging from the rubble weeping and waving a white flag, the survivors were outraged and more determined than ever to not only never surrender, but also to get a hold of the rascals responsible for this airborne hooliganism, and paste 'em a good one in the kisser.

By the end of World War I, bombs of more than a ton were being dropped by every side that had aircraft with which to drop them, and the path was cleared for the development of larger and more specialized bombs in World War II. The U.S. had progressed from the Mark III 50-pounder to the M34 2,000-lb., general-purpose bomb, which was dropped in prodigious quantities from the ETO to the PTO, and proved to be one ton of persuasion when released from bomb racks under fighter-bombers such as the Corsair and P-38 Lightning, or from the bomb-bay doors of the mighty B-17, B-24, and B-25. The British were leading the way with larger weapons such as the 12,000-lb. "Tall Boy" and the 22,000-lb. "Grand Slam," these last two meant to pierce the yards of protective concrete covering submarine pens up and down the European coast, at which job they excelled. There was also a breakthrough in the devilish science of incendiary devices, and clear-cut and ruthless plans about how to use them, such as the blistering firestorms that engulfed Dresden and Tokyo. In such events the city was set ablaze by a multitude of smaller fire bombs, which then combined their conflagrations to produce the dreaded firestorm, in which hurricane-force winds are generated and the entire city becomes its own funeral pyre as fresh air is sucked into the massive flames to replace the air rushing upward with the smoke and cinders. In old wooden cities this made for a vision of the apocalypse that has few equals in history ... at least until the U.S. put together the atomic bombs of August 1945, which flattened Hiroshima and Nagasaki on the Japanese mainland, and perhaps saved us the casualties and trouble of invading that bellicose nation. There is some evidence that Japan was already on the verge of collapse, and that we were keen on making a point about both Pearl Harbor and the entry of the Russians into the Pacific theater, but many authorities estimate that we were saved anywhere from 100,000 to half a million of our own troops killed and wounded if the assault on the mainland was anything like Iwo Jima and Okinawa.

Bombing with conventional explosives had not caused the German surrender in the spring of 1945; instead it had hardened resistance and their industrial output actually went up despite the efforts of the Army Air Force to pound them down with daring (and costly) daylight raids, while the British took over the night for their own, and could sometimes use the fires from our bombing runs to target their own nocturnal excursions. Be that as it may, we still had to cross the Rhine with tanks and infantry and take possession of the Thousand Year Reich ourselves to make their lunatic leader commit suicide and the German army see the light of reason. An important point, that one: bombing alone will not do the job.

We were to ignore this to our peril and disappointment during the Vietnam War. If ever there were a country as thoroughly bombed as Vietnam, it would probably no longer have a name or a geographic border. The Viet Cong were so determined to be the last ones standing that they used our B-52 bomb strike craters as classrooms and theaters for cultural presentations. And when we were done trying to bomb them back into the Stone Age (as General Curtis "Bombs Away" LeMay had termed his philos-

An F/A-18 Hornet gets shot into the air from the deck of the USS Nimitz, *laden with exploding options, including the AIM-9 Sidewinder air-to-air missile, RIM-7M Sea Sparrow radar-guided air-to-air missiles, Rockeye cluster bombs, and the AGM-88 High Speed Anti-radiation missile (HARM), which destroys enemy radar sites.*

ophy during an enthusiastic press conference), the efforts of millions of volunteers and draftees, and the sundering of a nation (ours and theirs) had taken place because we thought for a few years that with enough ill-will and heavy bombs, including deadly clinging napalm, we would be able to dictate to these relatively primitive (in our eyes) people what their future would be. Fifty-eight thousand American dead was the butcher's bill for the leaders who had forgotten history, or tried to use Detroit engineering to fix complex overseas problems.

Today the United States is still very keen on airpower and the projection thereof, and this is handy because we really haven't been threatened in the air for close to fifty years, making our slow

bombers perfectly safe to take their time and fly as high and leisure-
ly as they wish. We have also developed an entirely new generation
of so-called "smart bombs," although it should be noted that these
still have the ability to do dumb things like kill our own people and
hit the wrong target—they are "smart" only in the sense that we
now have all sorts of GPS (Global Positioning Satellite) technology
aboard them which can guide them to an almost exact coordinate
through fog, smoke, and haze. But also remember that these coordinates are only as good as the people who designate them on the
ground (with lasers or by pushing a set of numbers), and there's no
guarantee that the target will be at those coordinates when the
bombs and missiles arrive.

53

Bombs can be General Purpose, Fragmentation, Anti-armor, Demolition (which is more blast than fragments), as well as the awesome Big Blue, the Fuel Air Explosive known as the Daisy Cutter. This was first trotted out in Vietnam and used for clearing helicopter landing zones in the densest jungle, as well as for bombing the locals back into the Stone Age, but the Daisy Cutter was recently given a makeover and made heavier than ever (over 20,000 lbs.), and it can still be almost as devastating as a nuke, in that it will suck all the air out of any area it's dropped on (such as a cave complex), and will cause anyone under it to regret their choice of opposing our will—even if it doesn't lead them to surrender. The Daisy Cutter is actually not about surrendering—it's about dying.

We also have other Fuel Air Explosives for when we're really in a "no prisoners" mood. These work by exploding a mist that spreads into every gully and trench it encounters, as well as entering houses and cave mouths ... and then the mist is ignited.

Except for the B-52s that operate from many miles up, most fighter-bombers these days will deliver their loads from low down, ranging from one-thousand feet to right down on the deck. These modern attack aircraft can carry a wide array of bombing options, from the little Mk 20 Mod 2 475-lb. "Rockeye II" antitank cluster bomb to the M118 General Purpose 3,000 pounder, good for most any situation, from formal armies dumb enough to clump up where you can bomb them, to religious fanatics if they're caught together in a vulnerable place. Cluster

This is a modified 500-lb. penetrator bomb which has been hardened and thermally protected to increase the amount of time it takes to "cook off" in case of fire aboard a ship, such as the USS John C. Stennis. These can be loaded on either the F/A-18 Hornet or the F-14 Tomcat.

bombs do indeed throw out a cluster of bomblets that then each explode, extending the reach of any given bomb a great deal farther. We also have bombs with sensors on the noses, GPS capabilities, television cameras, and the ability to sense their proximity to a designated target such as a truck or a tank. The fuses run the gamut from precise time devices to the "all ways" fuse—this puppy is gonna explode no matter how it lands, upside down or backwards—boom!

Some of our newer bombs have a retarder to make them slow down as they reach the earth, which both gives the dropping airplane the chance to skedaddle, and also focuses the blast on the surface instead of the great weight and momentum carrying the whole shebang down into the earth. For that we have the new Bunker Buster, which is a clever ground-penetrating bomb used for underground complexes and, once again, those pesky caves. The Paveway bomb is a laser-guided monster that can follow a beam from the ground to strike precisely where we wish it to go, and Special Forces have become very fond of this capability, as it means they can point a special laser designator at whatever is giving them a problem, and make that problem go away in a New York minute. No muss, no fuss!

Rockets and Missiles

Rockets and missiles need to be kept separate, and the only way to do that is to understand what makes them streak across the sky like a thunderbolt from Zeus. A rocket has propellant contained within it, and when this is ignited Newton's third law of motion comes into play—basically, it will be going hell for leather in the opposite direction from where the flame is coming out. A missile has its own jet engine, and can be made quite a bit larger, making them the perfect platforms for launching nukes

Another system for fast deployment, the High Mobility Rocket System is shown here firing off a fast salvo. Able to fit in a C-130 Hercules, this is another way to give more punch to the fast-moving arms of our country's military.

over the North Pole, or sending astronauts to the moon. It is widely believed that the ancient Chinese invented the rocket around the tenth century, but lacking hard evidence we must follow what examples we can find, such as the bizarre Swedish rocket-spear of the 1500s. This can't have been much more than a frightening firework, but it was fired from a cannon, after which the rocket motor took over. As to whether it ever landed anywhere near the enemy, history records no wars in the 1500s that were decided by rockets. There were similar devices reported from India in the 1700s, but again nobody kept the kind of records we would like to see before putting together a good flow

chart of the rocket's history. A British officer of the early 1800s came up with (and named after himself) the Congreve Rocket, which was mounted in clusters on sort of a ladder and ignited at any number of primitive peoples from one end of the old Empire to the other. The Hale Rocket of the Civil War was given a good try-out, and was stabilized in flight by having its exhaust emerge in three directions in an attempt to impart spin as with the rifle bullet of the same era. And while such luminaries as Goddard and the very strange and brilliant Jack Parsons contributed to the advance of rocketry, it was the Germans in World War II who took the rockets everyone else was using and made the terrifying V2, that 28,000-lb. guided ballistic missile that carried a ton of high explosive into the hearts of London and Antwerp, to the tune of four thousand of them between September of 1944 and April of 1945.

The United States had been using rockets under the wings of fighter-bombers and as a replacement for the .50-caliber Browning machine gun on landing craft in the Pacific, but the new German weapons caught everybody's attention, to the point where we launched "Operation Paperclip," which was an attempt to snag every German scientist we could before our Soviet "allies" scooped them all in a bag and took them to Moscow. It might even be said that because of Operation Paperclip, the United States got to the moon first, not to mention winning the missile race of the 1950s and 1960s, because the links between the V2 and the Titan II are fairly close, except that the Titan has a 20-megaton warhead and can travel 9,300 miles from

This is a picture of the last Titan II being launched. Long the mainstay of Strategic Air Command, the mighty Titan was our first choice in the Cold War, and had enough range (5,500 miles) and accuracy to serve as a credible deterrent against the Reds.

its launch point. It's about a hundred feet tall and lives in silos quietly underground.

And yes, there is a great deal of rocket science involved with making these puppies fly. The thrust level can be adjusted by how the burning propellant is configured within the tube, and you can integrate a rocket with a ramjet engine, which, like all jet engines, as one old Navy instructor used to lecture, "the faster it goes, the faster it goes," this because jets take air in and then combine them with fuel, give them a spin through a turbofan on some models, and shoot the whole thing out the back even quicker than it came in. The combustion and thrust can be altered by how big a hole you put on the back end, and then what type of vanes you have to guide the explosive outpouring that marks the passage of your rocket or missile. You can also recombine the exhaust with more propellant to get an ever greater kick out the back, and there are clever ways of cooling the thrust nozzle, including the regenerative system whereby there are thin layers of fluid circulating within the thrust nozzle, each kept at a progressively lower temp until the whole unit is cooled down very gradually.

You can fire missiles from a concrete pad, or from a ramp with a rail (as aboard early subs like the USS *Growler*), from a tube, as in submarines and aboard ships, or from silos buried deep beneath the Iowa landscape, as well as other selected spots from North Dakota to Lop Nor in western China. There are three stages to the ignition, the first to get it off the ground, the second to boost it into the atmosphere, and the third to drive it onto the target all those miles away. And then you'll need to guide them, because nothing is more frightening than an unguided missile. Inside the brain of the missile will be an inertial platform that contains accelerometers (telling it how fast it is going) and gyros (no, not the Greek sandwich, but clever little tops that sense

which way is up), not to mention GPS sensors and a few classified widgets. A tiny computer will tweak the control surfaces and
the thrust nozzle to adjust the flight path as it progresses across
the heavens, and it will sense a bunch of other things, such as the
earth's rotation and the air temperature, which will affect its passage. Some missiles and rockets have heat sensors or electromag-
netic radiation sensing devices, making them head unerringly
toward things like the hot engine of an enemy jet. U.S. missiles
such as the SLCM and the ALCM (sea and air launched cruise
missiles, respectively) have a feature called Terrain Contour
Matching, where the computer aboard the missile has a map of
the enemy area with contours, and the missile can read them as
it goes and fly unerringly into the right valley and then out again.
This is not a simple or easy thing to design and place on every
missile. And guess what? You can't re-use them, either. It's a one-
way trip.

The ALCM and the Tomahawk are close brothers, using
the same basic makeup and having many of the same uses. If
you've watched television in the past two years you've seen plenty of Tomahawks, mostly launched at night by the U.S. Navy in
jaw-dropping displays of American might (which is meant to be
a subtle dig—some of them missed completely, some flew into
countries we hadn't declared war on yet, and some hit our own
people or planes—they don't always do just exactly what you tell
them to do). The Tomahawk has a turbofan engine that drives it
at around 500 mph; it has the terrain following feature as well as
GPS, and flies very low, and can shoot out about 1,500 miles with
an accuracy (on the best days) of mere feet. It weighs a svelte
3,200 pounds (like your Ford Taurus) and can be tipped with
everything from explosives to a 250-kiloton warhead, and that's
enough to end most civilizations on the spot, perhaps including
our own. At the other end of the scale we have the little 30-lb.

The USS Shiloh *launches a Tomahawk missile into Iraq. "Tomahawk" is a registered trademark, and the missile can fly for 1,500 miles at 550 mph, making it 18 feet and 3,500 pounds of diplomacy at the sharp end, all for a cost of $569,000 per shot. But it's cheaper and safer than using pilots.*

shoulder-launched Stinger missile, which can be passive infrared or active ultraviolet homing, meaning it's the end of most airplanes you fire it at. That would be great, if we were the only ones who had or used such systems, but we sold hundreds and thousands of them to the Taliban when they were whacking the Russians in Afghanistan in the 1980s, and guess what? Many of them, while still elderly, are still out there and still just as dangerous as when we first designed them. They can go up to better than a mile, and shoot sideways about three miles. The Russians also made their own "Grail SA (surface to air) 7," and the British made the Blowpipe (more of the same), and for all we

The Avenger weapons system is a short range (4.3 miles) air defense missile battery that fires Stinger missiles, and has a .50-caliber machine gun.

know there's an Indonesian version we haven't seen yet—but why design your own when there are thousands of these systems floating around out there? There have been thirty-four attacks with these on civilian airliners in the last twenty years, and about twenty-five of them succeeded according to the Associated Press.

The American rocket called the TOW is a tube-launched optically guided weapon. That means you fire it from your shoulder or a mount on a Hummer or Bradley, and as long as you keep the sight centered on the enemy's tank, that tank will be having a bad day in mere seconds. There are also fly-by-wire rockets that do the same thing, except they trail a long thin leash behind them to give them feedback about where the thing was aimed.

For shooting down airplanes we have the HAWK system, three pretty good missiles on a tracked vehicle. For attacking subs from helicopters there are the Subroc and Asroc. For use when you're not quite sure, the Asroc at 1,000 pounds becomes an acoustic torpedo once underwater; or the Subroc, which is 4,000 pounds of whup-ass, for use when you're really sure you have the latest enemy sub lined up and all ready to go to the scrap heap.

When there's a situation where only the largest missile will fill the need, they launch the Pershing (named for "Black Jack" Pershing, head of the AEF in World War I), which has a 450 kiloton warhead and can make almost anywhere into a shadow land. We have them on 18-wheelers, and they also take train trips to prevent hostile forces from targeting their silos.

Then, when the defense industry lobbyists get the better of you, we have the Patriot missile, which was meant to knock down incoming Scuds during the first Gulf War. First we were told it did just that, then we were told there were some problems, and now it appears that lighting a sparkler and waving it might have been as effective as using this hapless system. When Ike warned us about the threat from the military-industrial complex in his final speech, I think that things like the Patriot were what he had in mind. As it turns out, far more Scuds were destroyed on the ground by Special Forces using the Barrett .50-caliber rifle and laser-designated air strikes than were ever hit by any Patriot, despite the great name and stellar PR campaign. It's enough to make a military historian become a pacifist, especially when you take a gander at the price tag. And to think we could have used that money for housing, food, and education, or to train five hundred Navy SEALs!

A Scud launcher raises up prior to firing. These poorly made missiles were most effective as terror weapons, there being very little accuracy or durability built into them.

The infamous Patriot, which not only may have failed to destroy any Scuds in flight, but might have caused more damage by its actions in the air. This is the kind of help we don't need too much of in pursuing our national aims overseas.

Which brings us to the Star Wars missile defense system, which exists as a whiteboard concept only right now. This massive boondoggle has been described as "trying to hit one rifle bullet with another rifle bullet," and that may be a charitable description of its abilities. It appears that in opposition to almost every scientific analysis of this problem (spot the enemy missiles, put up your own to knock them down), we are going full speed ahead with this, and it is truly frightening to think that such a loopy concept could gain credence among respectable military men.

It should be noted that while I have the greatest respect for the men and women of our armed forces, I am tipped over into bitter contempt at companies that sell our country a bill of goods and walk away laughing. This is not only unethical, it goes against prudent military planning, and weakens our cause rather than strengthening our ability to face a hostile world with our chin up and a smile on our face that says "Don't tread on me."

Rockets and missiles will always have a place in our arsenal, and are in truth a pretty efficient way to smack people and things at a good distance. For attacking tanks and airplanes they are just excellent (but let's keep our stock to ourselves in the future, eh boys?), and the small lightweight systems such as the early LAWS (light antitank weapon system) were amazing breakthroughs in their day (the 1960s). This was the first disposable one-man rocket, based on the old WWII bazooka, but with a world of difference. To use it you took the ends off, popped up the sights and let 'er rip, and you could then put another round in and do it all again, or just huck it in the bushes if you had more

The AGM-86 is an air-to-surface strategic missile (shown here being loaded into a B-52—note the dummy rear-gunner position below the tail) made by Boeing, that can intelligently smite its targets while doing 550 mph.

The AIM-9 Sidewinder, our nation's workhorse air-to-air missile. It's a heat seeker that has a range of ten miles and costs $41,300 to make. Almost ten feet long, it uses an infrared system to target the opposing jet's engine and destroy it.

pressing and tactical needs closer at hand. Against bunkers and light tanks it was just great, and paved the way for some of the astonishing one-man weapons of today, such as the SMAWS. Perhaps in the future we'll have more of the cheap and innovative thinking that brought us the LAWS, and less of the pork-barrel mentality that has driven the Osprey, Crusader, and that silly Star Wars program. Or at least we'll have missiles and rockets that, when we fire them in times of great need, will be proven to work as they should.

An F-16 Fighting Falcon gets ready to go in harm's way, carrying two AIM-9 missiles as well as CBU-12 bombs, and a targeting pod. Using these modern-day bombs and missiles, this plane can protect itself in the air, and mash things on the ground with great precision.

CHAPTER 4

Over the Hill: Artillery

EVER SINCE THE FIRST warrior hurled the first rock at the first enemy, the idea of using a larger rock has loomed large. Or perhaps a faster rock was the answer? The ancient Greeks and their contemporaries had various slings that could be whirled around one's head and released (with some practice) at just the right moment to fly through the air and anger or even kill an opponent. One of the small stones used for this even had a somewhat childish motto carved on it: "Take That!"

There was also something called "Greek Fire," which seems to have been an early incendiary device, sort of napalm for the toga and sandal set. Various siege machines made their mark on these early conflicts, but it isn't until the invention of gunpowder that we can begin the history of artillery, and follow it up to the so-called "King of Battle," the modern U.S. artillery. However, the invention of gunpowder is one of those things that has been lost in the mists of time (or perhaps the gunsmoke of the centuries), and radiates rumor and myth like shrapnel. There is some general agreement that it was first brought to light in ancient China, and then migrated through India to the Middle East, where various factors such as the Crusades opened up the European market to this substance that was to forever alter the nature of warfare (and diplomacy for that matter, the best defense being a good offense, after all).

True to its somewhat mystical perception at the start, the friar Roger Bacon carefully encoded the formula for gunpowder as it came to him, this being one part sulphur, six parts saltpeter, and two parts charcoal. This remained the accepted mix until nitrocellulose was introduced in the 1840s, and it still will produce a goodly "bang!" In the early days gunnery was a form of magic, and perhaps black magic at that. It's pretty easy to see how such a reputation came into being; one can imagine the experiments that must have gone wrong along the way, reducing sundry alchemists' huts (and sundry alchemists) to flaming cinders in a twinkling.

But someone rightly thought that if you could contain the explosion of the gunpowder in a suitable (probably metal) container, it would be possible to make a round ball (of stone most likely) fly in the general direction of the enemy, and that the results might make one a duke or an earl, or, for the truly ambitious, a king. Or at least scare the daylights out of the other side. Our first picture of a cannon is recorded as having been drawn in 1326, so it only took eighty years for Bacon's formula to gain wide use; and twenty years after that the English had cannons in support of their knights and bowmen at Crécy.

From the early wrought-iron cannons, which were prone to bursting and wiping out one's own people almost as often as they managed to bowl over a line of knights or smash a castle wall, manufacturers began to cast their cannons in a variety of

Medieval cannon. Early artillery was a black art as much as a science, but here the gunners are using a quadrant to estimate the elevation of the cannon. Note that the barrel is made of strips bound together, like a wooden cask, and the wheels have been reinforced.

metals, including brass, bronze, iron, or whatever was lying around the shop. And by 1500 some of the reliability issues had been ironed out, producing a force with which to reckon. Castles that were not armed with cannons were now all but useless, unless you preferred to die among tapestries, and oar-driven galleys were forever swept from the ocean by the ship-mounted cannon, most notably at the massive battle of Lepanto in 1571. Both land and sea warfare had been altered for all time by this strange explosive force, and the more illuminated thinkers of the time busted their brains trying to discern how best to develop the cannon into something that was lighter and more effective. This is a theme of the inventions that were to follow.

Any fortifications that were now built (after about 1500) would have places in the walls for cannons, and some consideration of their field of fire. The great French designer Vauban (1633–1707) produced a series of plans and actual forts that grew ever more elegant, thrusting out spurs that could sweep their neighboring walls with shot, and there grew an entire science of the siege that involved digging complicated and sheltered ditches ever closer to the fort in question until your own artillery could be brought close enough to batter the walls and make a breach for the more enthusiastic members of the attacking party.

These early cannons were made with long metal strips for the barrel, these being bound by hoops of metal. As such, when you put too much black powder into the muzzle and shoved it to the back, put a big stone on that and touched the whole thing off, predictably there were some prodigious explosions that wrecked everything nearby, and made the other gunners reluctant to over-charge their pieces. Once guns were cast all of a piece, some of this danger was mitigated, but you can wreck any gun by jamming too much propellant into it even to this day.

The mortar and the howitzer made their first appearance in the 1600s. They are simple and related guns, meant to fire at a high angle over the tops of things like hills, trees, and castle walls. All guns started by being mounted on a heavy wooden frame, but this made for tough slogging when it came time to press forward. As a result, the field carriage came into being, this being two wheels on either side of the barrel and a long tail (known as the trail) to balance the critter as you aimed it in a rudimentary way, using handspikes to lever the muzzle toward the enemy, and place the cannon back at its starting point when the effects of recoil had shoved it back a few yards. Naval guns had simple mounts and small wheels, as it wasn't expected that they would have to be dragged from, say, Paris to Moscow.

Loading the cannon became a fine art, and had to be choreographed like a ballet to ensure that the maximum effectiveness was obtained from any one gun, much less a battery of the same. In this not much has changed, and it is worth considering that the planners of the M1A1 Abrams Main Battle Tank opted for a human loader over the mechanical version, surmising that a person was more flexible and attentive than any metal arm flinging a shell into the breech. To load the early muzzleloaders you first swabbed out the breech to make the sooty build-up less resistant, as well as to extinguish any lingering sparks from the last firing, which could ignite the fresh powder and make for one less cannon and perhaps five less men on your side. Then you had a fellow put his thumb over the hole in the top and at the rear of the barrel to prevent air from getting in that way (another safety precaution—and all of these came from hard and deadly experience) as you shoved with a rammer the powder charge (in premeasured bags as time went along) and then the shot into the muzzle. Then the gunner attempted to give the illusion that he was actually aiming this thing, by thinking about his last shot and observing the wind and such, and then on command a flame was put to the touch hole and the whole thing erupted, flinging itself backward, and your round was away.

After about 1500, metal replaced stone in making shot, and because it wasn't manufactured very precisely, the average gun wasn't overly accurate. If the shot was a bit smaller than the bore the effect would be a series of collisions with the wall of the interior of the barrel, resulting in the shot coming out and winging away toward the opposite direction from wherever the last hit took place. If the shot was too big it would generate tremendous friction on the inside of the barrel, and be prone to another of those tidy explosions among the gunners. None of this made for pinpoint shooting. As time went along the process of making the guns and the shot improved, and there was even a bit of science applied to how you aimed the darn thing. The angle of the barrel was pretty important, as you might guess, and the exact amount of powder played a significant role in how far and in what direction the shot flew. Solid shot was also augmented by such innovations as expanding shot (sometimes two balls linked

This droll illustration of artillery from the American Revolution leaves out a few things—such as the rest of the gun crew (that ball on the ground isn't going to teleport itself into the muzzle). And no matter how good a horseman that officer is, he will be walking after they touch the gun off and the horse bolts.

by a bar or chain that would spread out in flight to take down masts, sails, and rigging at sea) and canister or grapeshot. Canister was a bucket with metal balls in it that spread out when fired, and grapeshot was balls tied together that did much the same thing, producing an effect like a shotgun, and used for when the "whites of their eyes" were visible. This was known for tearing huge gaps in an advancing line of infantry, and reducing cavalry to dazed pedestrians. Explosive shot had also been tried a number of times, but it was always considered dangerous until a good fuse could be developed.

The first American artillery was whatever they could capture from the British or get from the French, and as such was a hodgepodge of types. But it is worth remembering that one of General Washington's first orders of business was to throw the "lobster back" redcoats out of the city of Boston, and to do that he employed the bookish Colonel Knox, one of the unlikely heroes of the American Revolution. In the fall of 1775, besides sending Benedict Arnold off on his doomed trip to Quebec through darkest Maine, Washington also asked Knox to go west to Ticonderoga, fetch the British artillery that had fallen into our hands as a result of Ethan Allen's capture of the fort (along with the ubiquitous Arnold), and bring the guns east to help dislodge the Brits. How Knox did this in the dead of winter on Indian trails across half-frozen streams is one of the great stories in military history. Knox himself had little military background, and was a rather stout and jolly fellow we are told, but he had run a bookstore before the war and his favorite subject was military history. Perhaps reading about Alexander the Great and Hannibal gave him a few notions of how to move across difficult terrain, but however he did it, the guns appeared on Dorchester Heights come spring, and as a result the British duly left The Hub. The first great American achievement with artillery had been accomplished by mobility, audacity, and surprise.

By 1800 the role of artillery was firmly established on land and at sea, and the fact that Napoleon was trained as an artilleryman and got his first good notices by using grapeshot on mobs in the streets of Paris bears some pondering. All of Napoleon's troops were known for their ability to move quickly and quite far, and they could also respond to things that came up in a very smart fashion, with the infantry and guns wheeling about to address a threat to the flanks in jig time. Roundshot was still the primary item fired out the front, and it traveled so slowly that it could be seen in flight, and rolled along the ground after landing before its motion was arrested, where it was still capable of taking off an arm or a leg. Napoleon's guns came in all types, but the 5.2 inch 18-pounder is a good example of a typical gun of the early 1800s. The "18-pounder" refers to the weight of the shot. There were also 24-pounder howitzers that used less powder, a slightly lesser weight shell, and were used to attack from a

A 12-pounder Napoleon, the classic Civil War cannon, with its caisson to the left (for carrying ammo). These cannon, double-shotted with canister, broke the back of Pickett's men at Gettysburg, firing pointblank.

high angle. A 12-pounder gun needed about two and a half pounds of powder to make it get up and whistle "Dixie."

    With the advent of the American Civil War, the United States became of necessity a warrior nation, and a good many of the half-million killed in that conflict were done in by native

American artillery, mostly of the 12-pound variety, although grapeshot and canister had prominent roles in smashing attacks such as General Pickett's ill-fated dash at the Union line at Gettysburg. Twelve-pounders of this era (known as "Napoleons" from Napoleon III who had a hand in the design) could shoot about two thousand yards, and took an amazing amount of soldiers to feed and transport. Eight gunners, six drivers, and twelve horses were needed. This was a lot of people, and a lot of horses, and a lot of food to feed them and carriages to ride them around to where they were needed. And once the other side saw where the artillery was located they were prone to firing their own guns at it, or using cavalry or light infantry to dash among the gunners and foment mayhem, which did nothing for the efficiency of a battery.

These were the last of the smoothbore muzzleloaders, and they were fussy to load and aim, and produced unbelievable amounts of smoke on the battlefield, so after the first few shots it was anyone's guess as to just where the shot was flying. Friendly fire has always been with us, and in the Civil War it came to be almost a trademark of some battles. It is debatable if the tragedy of dying in war is made lesser or greater by being shot by one's own people, but artillery could now make this more possible than ever. However, the artillery branch of the army had gone from an unreliable noisemaker to a respected and feared arm of warfare in a mere six hundred years.

The breechloading cannon was another product of the American Civil War, also in the 12-pounder version of about 3-inch caliber. For the first time a shell with all the propellant and shot included could be thrust in the back of the gun (in later models), and then when it ignited it engaged threaded grooves on the inside of the barrel known as "rifling" which imparted a spin to the shell in flight, much like a good football pass, and this stabilized its passage through the air. This innovation made for much more accurate guns, as well as increasing their range, and the artillery began its ascent to the pinnacle of deadliness.

To use these new guns, one could employ direct or indirect fire. Direct fire was pretty simple: spot the target and shoot straight at it over open sights; observe the fall of shot; manhandle the gun back to the original position; and try again. If they did hit anything using this method it would be torn asunder in no time. But those guns were also quite noticeable on the battlefield, not only because of the effect of their firing but also because of the crashing noise and clouds of smoke, and this would attract unwanted attention from enemy guns and small arms, to say nothing of the obstreperous cavalry who always seemed to "ride to the sound of the guns," which doesn't mean they wished they had an 8-track of famous barrages, but rather that the artillery was always a plum target. Nobody has ever been shelled by artillery without using that time-honored expression: "Where the hell is THAT coming from?"

This brings up another option, which is the modern way, and is called indirect fire. For this maneuver, a bright-eyed and intrepid observer is placed in a hopefully sheltered spot, and then after a few shots are tried, he reports back on how accurate they are. This was by semaphore and telegraph in the early days, and by radio today. Making little adjustments from side to side isn't hard, but getting the right range is a very tricky business, and for this there is a clever and logical method. The two things to avoid are "short" (which may mean among your own troops) and "over," which might strike a few mules and tents behind the target, but isn't getting you any closer to them waving the white flag. If the first shot is short, you then make a bold correction so that the next shot is over, and then just alternate between additions and subtractions until the target is in the midst of an explo-

Krupp's Big Bertha. One of the legendary guns that launched WWI by pounding Belgian forts into rubble. The wheels made for use in mud, such as, oh, say anywhere from the English Channel to Switzerland from 1914 to 1918, are clearly visible.

sion. This is called "bracketing," and relies on keeping good track of what the angles and charges were for each shot, thus enabling you to increase or lessen the angle and powder so as to whack the bad guys where they live in the most efficient way. No artillery piece is accurate enough to place a shell in the exact same spot more than once, but you can get darn close with good observers and well-trained batteries of guns.

Frederick the Great was the first to mass his artillery into batteries, and Napoleon carried the concept further so that there was a flow chart to his battles that you could almost count on.

They started with a barrage, which is a curtain of fire, and then went to area bombardment of troops. This method is still used today, and indeed the brightest spot for artillery (if one of the darkest for mankind) was World War I, which saw the mighty guns come to the fore in a way that shattered many preconceptions, as well as not a few bodies and minds. The fantastically large guns of the Krupp Company began by smashing the Belgian forts at Liege into dust, prompting their surrender, and from there it was almost an artillery war with some machine guns, gas, infantry, and airplanes thrown in to make it more grisly. The barrages of World War I have passed into legend, no doubt because of their deadly effect, but also for the fact that more guns were grouped more closely together than at any other time in history, and some of the preliminary bombardments went on for a week straight. Even so, given the perversity of warfare, high explosives and shrapnel weren't very good at cutting barbed wire, meaning that the Poor Bloody Infantry were often hung up on their way across No Man's Land, and this made them easy pickings for the machine guns and artillery of the other side. You really have to read the firsthand accounts of the battles of the Somme and Verdun to get an idea of how awful this endless artillery festival could be, and it may be no coincidence that the first studies of shell shock date from this time, although there was a "soldier's sadness" that had been noted in the Civil War. The fact that this walloping great hunk of metal could fall on you in a seemingly random fashion at almost any time did very little to promote mental hygiene.

By then, of course, the breechloader had swept everything before it, leaving the lowly mortar as the only muzzleloading artillery piece on the modern battlefield. Various breeches had been perfected, including that perennial favorite with adolescent students of guns, the "French Interrupted Screw" breech,

Here is the wonderful French 75mm, showing the interrupted screw at the breech, and a portable wine cellar... actually, an ammunition caisson set up and ready for rapid loading. American artillerymen used this cannon to fine effect, and it served right into World War II.

which revolved in a series of grooves to provide a tight seal and prevent the waste and leaking of gases on ignition. Perhaps the name in its mother tongue provokes fewer snickers. The French 75mm gun was the one to beat, and the United States used plenty of them once they set out to make the world safe for democracy, including a young battery commander named Harry S. Truman from Missouri.

Guns were lined up in France and Belgium wheel to wheel, and masses of shells were laid nearby, and when the order came down the gun crews started working them like they were earning overtime in hell. They might begin by pounding the rear lines to isolate the front trenches, and then move up to pound those, and then set up a rolling barrage that they hoped their troops would advance just behind. Needless to say, there were more than a few cases where troops were nailed by their own

The forward two turrets of a WWI Dreadnought, with old-fashioned observation towers and the ability to steam about pretty quickly and drop many tons of lead on opposing vessels, if they can be found. As at the Battle of Jutland in 1916, this sometimes proved harder than you might think.

guns, and the French supposedly even used their 75s to execute some of the mutineers of 1917 by simply assigning them to march to a certain set of coordinates and then shelling the tar out of that coordinate.

Naval guns had also expanded to meet the great ranges at which battles were now fought, such as at Jutland where the two sides caught only the barest glimpse of the other. But it was not until the 1920s and 1930s that 16-inch guns began to be mounted to ships, and these made it possible to throw a shell the weight of a Volkswagen out way past the horizon, which would cause no end of trouble for whoever was under it when it fell back to earth. There were also large railway guns that shelled from special tracks, and the so-called German "Paris Gun" that was able to lob fairly small shells smack into the middle of the City of Light from seventy-four miles away, by use of the lessened friction of the upper atmosphere and taking the rotation of the earth into account. Firing at airplanes also became a new occupation of the gunner, and for this various complicated sights were developed to predict where the plane would be by the time the shell got there—if he maintained his course and speed, which pilots soon learned to not do under any circumstances. Indeed, World War I was not only a watershed in artillery development, but also gave them no end of new things to shoot at, such as tanks and coastal forts.

By the time World War II rolled around, U.S. artillery was among the best in the world, both on land and at sea, largely due to the establishment of schools at places like Fort Sill, Oklahoma

An Airborne howitzer in full recoil as American paratroopers battle their way to Carentan, Normandy, in 1944. They all react to the noise in their own way, but this is a sure way to go deaf.

A massive 240mm cannon prepares to send many hundreds of pounds of lead downrange, sticking its snout out from under camouflage netting designed to fool the Luftwaffe in Italy, early in 1944. This was the "king of the battlefield," and looks it.

(where the 15,000-acre site was deemed large enough for almost any gun), and various naval gunnery establishments up and down both coasts. Naval gunnery also had men who would go ashore with the first waves of attacking troops and report back on the fall of shell to the ships, and there were few more dangerous jobs available. Direct fire still had its place, as in the legendary

U.S. Navy destroyer that came in so close to the beaches at Normandy on D-Day that it almost grounded, but was able to pound the German positions with its 5-inch guns most successfully. Communications were always a problem, even after the development of the walkie-talkie, but at least now the observers had a small box they could yell into when the rounds were falling shorter and shorter. For the first time airplanes were used in an organized fashion to report on the effect of artillery fire, and this trend has continued to the present day. Artillery played a notable role in World War II, Korea, and Vietnam, where for the first time helicopters were used to establish batteries deep inside enemy territory—which wasn't hard, because it eventually became clear that the whole country was enemy territory. Be that as it may, Special Forces could sometimes be supported in remote jungle clearings by big guns, and when you're short of everything but the enemy, one appreciates the efforts of the "gun bunnies" to have their say about the outcome of an ambush.

Present-day Artillery

Today's U.S. Army field artillery is a force that has one foot in the past and one in the future. They still have their school at Fort Sill, but today there are subtle nuances that never came up before, although they are rooted in every artillery action that has ever taken place. First of all, as the pace and mobility of modern warfare has accelerated, the artillery has needed to develop the abil-

Having jammed the shell into this 155mm howitzer, the next step will be making sure the thing is pointed the right way and awaiting the order to "Fire!" The odd looking protrusions on the soldiers' helmets indicate they are in a war game, and if an enemy shoots them with special lasers, they will be "dead."

The latest in mobile artillery, the 105mm howitzer is relatively light (note the hollow tubular carriage), and ranges out many miles with modern ammunition. This is meant to give paratroopers some serious "bang!" in their usual forward (and pushing ahead) positions.

ity to move with the attacking troops, and to do this we have all manner of self-propelled gun, these being a marriage between a tank and an artillery piece. One indication of the modern age was the introduction of the self-propelled gun, such as the 155mm (SP) howitzer, which has the usual features of a howitzer (shorter barrel, less propellant) in a 6.1-inch gun, and can roll right along at 34 mph, making it a pretty speedy rig for such a conglomeration of hostile intent. It has a range of about 16,000 yards, and can fire a wide selection of shells, from standard high explosive to chemical and nuclear rounds. Like its fellow tracked battle mate, the M1A1 Abrams Main Battle Tank, it can fire one shell at a high angle and then switch quickly to a fast low-angle shell, and arrange it so that both rounds arrive at the same time, doubling the destruction at the end point.

There are certainly still towed guns, which need a truck or larger vehicle to get them close to the danger, such as the M102 and the M101A1, which can boost a shell about six miles away, but these days the preference seems to be for self-propelled models such as the M109A1, M107, and M110A1. There is a great deal more maintenance to be done when you graft a really big gun onto a tank, but these still find employment where there is need of a serious rain of shot and shell while also having the ability to press forward. They have crews of between four and six men, and it takes about a half hour to get everything ready to go. They can also be buttoned up against chemical and biological attacks, but not in what is considered any degree of comfort. Modern guns are still fired either as a barrage (which is like a curtain of explosions) or in concentration mode, where you pick a speck on the map and decide to render it unlivable, and hopefully the enemy was just taking their afternoon tea right at that spot. But on the modern battlefield, wouldn't a nice flight of Apache helicopters and/or A-10s be an even faster and more decisive response to the enemy's choice of tea spots?

But while the barrages of old have been to some extent replaced by air power and missiles, the use of a good large gun remains a solid choice on the modern battlefield, particularly if you can add range and mobility to their hulking bulks. Thus, the survival of the muzzleloader in the form of the mortar, which fires a shell at a high angle and does so without a lot of sound or smoke.

Above: A loader loading an 81mm mortar round, doing his thing in support of the soldier who sights the mortar and the commander's orders. Mortars remain the only muzzleloading artillery piece in the modern arsenal, and are great for indirect fire. The item on the key chain is either a rabbit's foot or a chemical weapon detection sensor.

Mortars are great for attacking lone outposts, because only the very clever will be able to discern the direction from which the threat is coming. The way you do this is to analyze the remainder of the shell in the ground after it explodes, and then send your own mortars back with an answer. Currently for mortars the United States has the 81mm and 107mm, and these are fairly heavy at seven hundred pounds, but can throw their 33-pound shells out about six thousand yards, making them handy as light artillery that you can get into place more quickly than the big guns.

It has to be noted, however, that we may be seeing a change in the future use of artillery. While big guns are deemed a great way to slaughter the enemy, they are heavy and expensive and can get out of sorts without the proper maintenance. The Pentagon has just

Showing just how big the 81mm mortar is—at least three men are needed just to carry the base, mount, and tube. After a couple more shots the base will be flat on the ground.

91

Crusader. A proposed self-propelled howitzer system that would be perfect if our enemies holed up in castles, or clumped up in a location where we could shell them night and day. But they don't and this was wisely cancelled.

junked the Crusader on the grounds that it is too heavy, can't be air-lifted, was designed for a war that never happened (the Russians pouring through the Fulda gap), and is the wrong horse to back in light of the nature of the current conflicts we find ourselves embroiled in at this writing. This decision was met with cries of dismay, particularly in the congressional district that was to have man-ufactured the Crusader, but it does seem to be rather too much of a good thing, and at far too high a price, to fight an enemy who prefers not to be shelled and demonstrates this by not presenting any sort of clear target. Most of the guns of the U.S. artillery are at least forty years old, and many of their roles on the battlefield have been taken over by tanks, airplanes, and missiles, and when fighting a global battle against terrorist groups, they seem unlikely to mass together in the sort of target that warms the artilleryman's heart. History would seem to dictate that it is unwise to throw away such a proven killer of enemies and winner of battles, but there may be less opportunity to employ the big guns in future conflicts than at any time since the Dark Ages. Hardly anyone holes up in a fortress any more, and massed barrages are for the most part these days more and more taken over by the Air Force, who can drop a greater variety of bombs with greater accuracy than the most perfect can-

This handy tactical radar system will track any incoming ordinance and give you a reading on the range and bearing—handy for mortar attacks; and it can also pick up shells as small as .50-caliber, excellent for counterbattery fire missions.

A sergeant of the 82nd ("All American") Airborne sights his howitzer carefully through a panoramic telescope for a howitzer at Baghdad International Airport. This also illustrates one of the weak points of artillery—if you can sneak into where they keep these guns, that telescope is pretty fragile.

non. It could well be that in the future we will turn Fort Sill into an open-air warehouse for our guns, although there might come a time when there will again be need for the offspring of Roger Bacon, and the cry will go out: "Fire for effect!"

CHAPTER 5

By Tire
and Tread:
Tanks

IN SEPTEMBER OF 1916, in an attempt to break the bloody deadlock of trench warfare on the Western Front of World War I, the British rolled out their new juggernaut: the tank. While the restless Mr. DaVinci had foreseen a circular wagon with guns many centuries before, this was the first use of tanks in wartime, and proved to be a great disappointment. The name "tank" was an attempt to disguise the true nature of the weapon, as early planners surmised that German intelligence might grow wary if they came across mention of a "chariot of the apocalypse," or a "war wagon tractor." While these early armored hulks were terrifying to the unlucky German soldiers caught in their path, many of them broke down (some before reaching the battle) or became mired in the ditches and shell holes that littered that pockmarked battlefield. At Cambrai in November of 1916, the British were able to throw four hundred tanks at the German lines, but again the result was hardly commensurate with the effort expended. However, eighty-five years of development would result in an entirely different beast—a rolling gun platform that could destroy anything in its path.

The trail to modern tank warfare is a long and winding one. Keep in mind that the cavalry in 1914 was waiting for the "Poor Bloody Infantry" (PBI) to finish whatever their tawdry scuffle in the mud was, so that the gentlemen (read: "cavalrymen") could ride forward and win the war as they had mostly been doing since the invention of the stirrup. It would be a long time before some of the diehards would come to accept the use of internal combustion engines for warfare. Even then, there are some echoes of class consciousness in the use of Rolls Royce armored cars in Mesopotamia during World War I—one may as well ride in style, after all, old boy! But, just as with the later Rolls Royce Merlin engine that powered the best fighter planes of World War II, Rolls simply had the very best machine for the job at hand. In time, some of that old cavalry spirit would be transferred to the clanking cacophonous creatures we call tanks, and eventually even the swift and hard-striking mobility of "Light Horse Harry" Lee (Robert E. Lee's father and a famed leader of horsemen in the American Revolution) and Bedford Forrest (Confederate cavalry genius who supposedly said that in war he wished to "get there first with the most") would settle like a mantle of honor over the turrets and exhaust stacks of modern armor. It still takes a fair amount of gumption and grit to be the leading edge of an assault and to be ever ready to "ride to the sound of the guns," just as cavalrymen had been doing for centuries.

American tanks had a tangled path on their way to becoming the "king of the killing zone." A WWI photograph of General (then Colonel) George S. Patton in France is a telling record, in that he is standing next to a French Renault FT 17 tank, adopted because we couldn't make enough or good enough units for our deployment in World War I. Already, as the commander of the U.S. 1st Tank Brigade, Patton displayed his shy and retiring nature by telling his troops in writing to always keep pushing forward, no matter what, and that the message he wished to send to the enemy was that "AMERICAN TANKS DO NOT SURRENDER."

Our tanks of the 1930s were pathetic little beasts, strapped as they were by budgetary shortfalls and our historic peacetime loathing for weapons. But, in the time-honored American way, once we determined that we were in World War II, the amazing might of industrial production came to the fore

The mighty Sherman tank, one of the American wonder weapons that secured victory in Europe during World War II. With a 75mm main gun, it didn't have the punch of the heavy German tanks, but it was reliable and simple, and was made in such vast numbers (49,000) that no country in the world could keep up with it. It was also known as the "Ronson," due to its proclivity for going up in flames like the famed cigarette lighter of the 1940s.

and began turning out more and better tanks than had ever been seen before. While the mighty German Mark IV, Panther, and Tigers were better made and had a more powerful gun (the ubiquitous and mighty 88mm), and while the Soviet T-34 is an all-time rough-and-ready classic, America went straight down the middle and produced many more pretty good tanks including the Stuart and the Sherman.

The Cold War was a time of frenzied preparation for what was assumed would be the tank battle to end all tank battles, hinging on the Fulda Gap and encompassing the entire European continent. The expectation was that the Soviets would roll a gajillion of their ever-improving but still basic tanks across the landscape heading west, and the job of the NATO forces was to act as a human tripwire and slow down the Communist tidal wave long enough for us to marshal some sort of response, nuclear if need be. As a result, American tank design focused on preparing for this massive battle, because the wars in Korea and Vietnam, while certainly having their share of proud and valiant armored participants, were mostly fought by infantry, artillery, and airpower.

Modern Tank Combat

Tanks have evolved amazingly over the years, and while the German blitzkrieg was history's first taste of fast moving, hard-hitting modern warfare, the Americans had sufficient time and chances to hone their act to a fine edge. The first thing you need to know is that tanks are cranky mechanical beasts that guzzle fuel and have a comfort level approaching the absolutely ungodly. When entering a tank, the sequence is as follows: first you bump your knee, then you bump your elbow, and lastly you bump your head. Repeat this until you want to write a proposal for a tank with foam insides—just make sure it isn't flammable. When the inside of the tank catches fire, everybody is about all done. It's not a question of "Gee, I wonder if all this fuel and ammo will ignite?" but rather what the size of the explosion will be. Many tanks do burn without exploding, but nobody is happy at the sight except the enemy. This has driven the development of such amazing technologies as Chobham reactive armor, which, while still classified, seems to come in bricks or plates that you affix to the outside (doing nothing for the aesthetics of the beast) and that blow outward at such a high rate of reaction as to neutralize the incoming shell or rocket.

In tank warfare, they don't send them out on their own unless they wish to park them at intersections as a helpful prod toward law and order among an unruly populace. For war fighting, tanks always work in platoons or "troops" or "squadrons," and that means clumping like models together, or setting up a mix of models suitable to the situation. So a modern American standard option would be the Abrams out front in a goodly number, followed by Bradley Fighting Vehicles (carrying some troops as well as being fast and having a 25mm gun), then the Combat Engineer vehicles, then the missile launchers, and then the fuel and maintenance and wreck-recovery vehicles, and a bunch of Hummers and plain old trucks, including Dodge pickups just to remind the troops of the local Quicky Mart back home. They can jigger this around in a number of ways, like shooting the Combat Engineers up front to deal with obstacles, but having the heavy guns out front always gives the option of hammering anything they meet (from other tanks or vehicles to bunkers and fortified positions) into the ground like the fist of Odin.

Tanks can proceed in line abreast, or follow one after the other. In the latter case, the procedure is much like a Special Forces patrol, in that there is a point man (tank), then each following tank covers left or right alternately, and the drag tank keeps an eye peeled behind for unwelcome tag-alongs. Tanks can also proceed into danger by having half the team get into a covering position to make sure the other half can move forward, at which point the dancers trade places and keep pushing ahead warily.

The tank commander is the key chap in the vehicle, as he is supposed to have a grasp on both what is happening outside (contact with the enemy, orders to go forward, retrograde movement [also known as "retreating"], or "Full Stop") as well as monitoring the mechanical soundness of his ride, keeping an eye on the fuel and ammo, and bringing his guns to bear on whatever falls within his purview. This is a pretty hard job. Israeli tank commanders were famous for exposing the top half of their bodies so as to have a better grasp of the battlefield, but they paid the price in dead tank commanders. Why wear a tank into battle if it isn't going to protect you? As Bill Mauldin puts it in a World War II Willie and Joe cartoon as his dogfaces are digging a trench: "I dunno ... it just seems that a moving foxhole attracts the eye." You don't need to worry about being ignored in a tank.

Tanks have an amazing psychological effect due to their noise and size, and the terror of shooting at one and not stopping it must be akin to being stuck in a bad slasher movie where they can never quite kill the monster. When that rumbling comes up over the horizon, even hardened infantry has been known to go weak kneed. Just the same as racking the slide on a Colt .45 or working the pump on a 12-gauge Mossberg, the sound alone may be enough to make poorly trained soldiers quail and civilians commit to staying on the sidelines.

The driver's job is to steer and work the throttle and brakes, and they better have had some practice with all three, as well as good eyes for what is and isn't suitable terrain. Failure to spot mud and marshland can result in the mobile battle platform becoming a fixed position, known in the trade as a "sitting duck." In World War II it was assumed that, as one old veteran puts it, "Any American kid could hop into any vehicle he encountered, turn the key and roar off." But it should be noted that this same veteran (a naval officer assigned as liaison with the U.S. Army in North Africa) managed to throw the tread off a Stuart tank, making for a lot of bad comments and hours of work to set it right. Take the corners too fast in those old tanks, and that's what happened.

The gunner will operate the main cannon, and is responsible for setting up and firing that thing (sometimes with the help of a loader) at the right target when requested to do so—and not before or after. It's a finicky job, and one where being ahead of the game is crucial. You don't want to hear your commander order: "Fire!" while you're fumbling around and wondering if you packed extra shells, and if so, where?

All armored vehicles work about this way, or in close variations of the foregoing. There will always be radio contact between tanks, and it will always be a hot and dirty job—hotter if you button it up in Iraq during the summer because of chemical, biological, or nuclear threats. And remember that there may be enemy helicopters firing missiles, or troops on the ground with powerful antitank missiles, or minefields—you can't afford to get a swelled head and assume you will be able to conquer everything. But despite the prediction that tanks are past their prime, some form of them is likely to be with us for a very long time. The improvements will be in armor, gun, and power plant technology, and the search for ever greater mobility.

The Abrams

By 1985 the M1A1 Abrams was the latest and greatest of all tanks ever made, and its staggering capabilities were only matched by its skyrocketing costs and incredible use of fuel. At about four and a half million dollars a pop, the Abrams is not the sort of vehicle that encourages you to forget where you parked it. It doesn't do very well in little city streets or on the rough terrain of places like, oh, say Afghanistan. But in its proper place, such as a desert, it is a truly awesome machine that can flatten anything it comes up against, from the Soviet-designed T-72 to a column of trucks. It bristles with technology and space-age "gee whiz!" additions, and can operate almost anywhere you can get the fuel tankers to fill 'er up.

There isn't a plant somewhere that just spits fully equipped M1A1s out the side door. In the modern world of United States weapons, they first began by reading what some policy wonk who's never been in a tank wants in a tank, then they began canvassing friendly countries and companies for the appropriate technology, went back and read their spec sheet again, and then commenced to shoehorning all the components together in the best way they could. While Leonardo could wake up from a nap and sketch out his vision, today's weaponry visions have to be the result of multiple visions. And if you think designing a massive killing machine using a committee is an easy task, you need to get out more.

"It's got to be massively heavy!" cry the cloistered Poindexters, "But not TOO heavy!" This process involves adding things and then subtracting things, sometimes together. "Put the biggest gun on it that we can find!" Okay ... howzabout this 120mm German-designed smoothbore cannon? It only sticks out

The M1A1 Abrams, probably the best tank in the world right now. It can shoot farther, withstand more abuse, and cruise faster than anything else out there. Note the improvised tread armor covering one of its weak spots—the complicated and easy to bung up bogie wheels that run the treads. With a 120mm main gun and a .50-caliber machine gun, the Abrams spells trouble for any other armored vehicle it meets—but it cannot win a guerrilla war.

fifteen yards over the bow. "It has to use multifuel—we have no idea what gas we can get for it." All right. "And you have to be able to button it up against noxious gasses and invisible radiation." Sigh ... "Not too tall!" One sort of wonders how these things get done at all, but they do get done, and often the result is amazing. Such is the case with the M1A1 Abrams.

A good view of the M1A1 Abrams showing just how long the 120mm main gun actually is, and the angled armor of the turret meant to throw off most antitank missiles.

The Abrams (named for General Creighton Abrams, a legendary armored commander) is the Main Battle Tank (MBT) of the United States, and we make a slightly lesser version for export to friendly countries. General Dynamics, the huge corporation, is the main supplier through their Land Systems Division. It has a 1,500-horsepower multifuel gas engine that is fully automatic (no gear grinding here!), featuring four forward gears and two reverse, depending on how fast you wish to go ahead or pull back. At twelve feet wide it's not going to fit into most airplanes or garages. At sixty-seven tons you will want to eyeball most Third World bridges long and hard before rolling across them, and it will cause a fair amount of damage to any but the best built roads. Depending on your driving style (drag racing and stop-and-start are the things to avoid), it can go about 280 miles before the needle hits "E." Offroading is no problem! As a matter of fact, they thought about that, and built in a 19-inch clearance to avoid scraping the underside (which is also armored against land-mines). It can cross a 9-foot wide ditch and climb a 60-degree slope—slowly. And if you open it up, it can do about 42 mph, which is a sure way to get the needle to drop like a stone on the gas gauge. But if you're bashing through the willywags (also know as "cross-country") better not count on cracking 30 mph.

Four lucky stiffs get to ride this thing around: a commander, a driver, a loader, and a gunner. They have a variety of sensors to help them in the tasks, and all the communication gear anyone could want. They can talk to each other, other tanks, men on the ground, and airplanes overhead, all of which is helpful once the bullets start to fly. They can see in the dark and through smoke and dust with infrared and heat-sensing viewers, and God help any target they spot, because that 120mm main gun can reach out and smack things up to two and a half miles away. It can also do this while on the run because of modern systems that detect and adjust for the motion of the tank as well as the movement of the enemy, while also figuring wind (no more of that "It's blowing from the east … I'll just aim off a bit"), cant (if the tank is tilted, as it almost always is), and even such arcane factors as ammunition temperature (because rounds fly differently if they're hot or cold). This isn't your grandfather's "Kentucky windage" shooting. Modern tanks are so clever that if you really don't like someone you can determine the range to them (through a laser range finder), fire one shell on a high mortar-like trajectory, and then quickly switch to a fast flat shot and actually have both rounds arrive at the same time on the unlucky object of your hostility.

The shells that can be fired through the main gun include kinetic rounds that use their own momentum to pierce other armor, and chemical rounds that come in a range of flavors. Rather than simply making the gun bigger and bigger to deal with thicker enemy armor, there are shells that can set up a shockwave and drive a chunk off the inside of the enemy's turret, which is deemed just as effective as putting the shell itself inside, and clever shells that can focus a thin jet of superheated gas that penetrates just enough to light up everything inside. Indeed, there is anecdotal and troubling evidence that someone has found a new way to do this—and use it against at least two of our AFVs in Iraq.

But, as hard as it is to realize, the 120mm isn't the only option, nor is it always the best option. The commander has an M2 .50-caliber machine gun, and the loader has an M240 7.62mm one, both right there above their hatches. And that's sort of a problem, because to use them they have to A) have the hatch open, and B) put their frangible bodies out in the open to fire the machine gun. The Israelis learned to their sorrow that while a tank commander may have a better overall vision of the battlefield by popping up and out, he is in no way as armored or protected in that position as when he is buttoned up and down in h. tank. Nevertheless, they may need those machine guns if they're up against infantry or trucks, or engaged in urban warfare. And a .50-caliber machine gun is not to be sniffed at, with a range of more than a mile and a massive bullet.

On the outside of the turret are smoke launchers if they need to mask their movements, and the amazing Chobham reactive armor. This system can actually react so quickly to an incoming round that it blows outward, dissipating the effect of the enemy round quite effectively. There is also a "cold spot" on each side so that friendly tanks can see through their infrared that they don't want to be involved in a "friendly fire" incident. They can also use the engine to generate smoke, and do so without letting the engine run out of oil, which isn't possible in a '62 Rambler.

Jam all those components together and you have the best tank ever built—but not without a few caveats. The irony of fighting wars that are essentially about control of oil by the use of a behemoth that gets one mile to the gallon bears some pondering. The M1A1 (and its improved version, the logically named M1A2) is a brilliant platform from which to fight wars, of the type it is good at fighting. For this they will want the room to run and maneuver, hills that aren't too darn steep, an enemy who has armor and trucks (because guerrilla forces won't come anywhere near you in this thing) and is dumb enough to engage them, and enough gas to keep the treads turning. Also the tanker trucks full of multifuel are not only not armored very well, but also have a tendency to disappear in a fireball when faced with RPGs and incendiary rounds that the Abrams would shrug off like gnats in June. The MBT isn't going to fit in most airplanes except the C17 Globemaster (which can just squeeze one of them in), so a good port city with loading facilities is needed as is a few weeks to get them anywhere at 30 mph average.

o M2-A2 Bradley Fighting
s lurking in the Karbala Gap
of Iraq. These are from the 3rd
nfantry Division. Note the lou-
ered sections on the sides—these
are "cold spots" to help friendly
forces spot them through thermal
imaging equipment to prevent
"blue on blue" as the British term
it—our "friendly fire." The 25mm
M242 Automatic Gun is shown, as
well as the rear hatch. The Bradley
reminds some viewers of the old
Stuart M3 light tank of WWII, but
the Stuart didn't have an infantry
squad inside the rear!

But if you can overcome the logistics of delivery and
resupply, the M1A1 Abrams tank is going to sweep everything
before it, and that's no mean feat on a modern battlefield. Even
the latest Ukranian T-90 is well advised to slink off once the
Abrams enters the field of battle.

The Bradley Fighting Vehicle

During the Vietnam War the steady and reliable old M113 APC
(armored personnel carrier) was a mainstay, although it was slow
and confined to mostly road patrols. It occurred to some of the
more visionary members of the military that a new APC would
be a good idea, one that could move faster, hit harder than the .50
caliber on the M113, and carry troops protected behind armor
until they were needed to deploy in the field. The result of this
thinking was a lot of head scratching, but eventually, after almost

ten years, the Bradley Fighting Vehicle emerged. Named for legendary World War II General Omar Bradley, in time 6,800 of these quick and lethal machines would be turned out, and their record for reliability, fast movement, and rapid shooting is a testament to the success of the lengthy selection and design process.

The Bradley can roll on its treads at up to 40 mph, and has a range of about two hundred miles. Its 25mm Boeing M242 Bushmaster chain gun is a very quick-firing cannon of proven lethality, and can chew the tar out of most trucks it runs into, to say nothing of enemy troops. It also has two TOW ATGWs, which give it an antitank punch out of all proportion to its size, which is about half the length of an Abrams and one-third the weight. But this shrinkage means it can also be jammed in a C-130, so it is far more deployable at a moment's notice than the Abrams.

Three crewmen operate the Bradley, a commander, a driver, and a gunner. The driver is in the front left of the hull,

This shot shows why tanks don't engage in street fighting if they can avoid it. This Bradley is moving away from the photographer, but the turret is turned all the way around and the commander is up out of his hatch with an M4 carbine at the ready. This is a tough way to operate. Also shown here is a clear view of the back hatch options, which include the oval door, the entire square hatch (which can lower and disgorge everyone), and the firing ports.

shoehorned in with the engine, while the commander and gunner share the turret, and up to six fully equipped infantrymen ride in the back, where they can spring out if the mood strikes them through a large ramp door, or through an escape hatch on the roof of their compartment. Escape hatches are much-desired features on all armored vehicles, due to the flammability issue mentioned before, which the British term cozily "brewing up." The infantry can fire their weapons from within the passenger compartment, through airtight firing ports that have their own built-in viewing periscopes.

A frontal view of the Bradley that shows the driver's turret below the main gun, hardened headlights, and the towing points under the nose for those deep sand traps. In the background to the left is a MedEvac M113, still rumbling along forty years after entering service.

The Bradley can be had in a number of configurations, from a sporty command model to a MedEvac version to a multiple missile launcher. With updated navigation and sensors such as infrared and thermal imaging, and the ability to become amphibious quickly, the Bradley has proven it's worth in two go-rounds against the Iraqis as a fine compliment to the M1A1 (and A2) Abrams. Their role is to transport squads forward in an armor assault in relative safety and comfort, and with constant upgrades it is likely that they will serve for a few more years as a proven hard charger in any armored brigade.

The USMC's pride and joy—the AAAV, for some reason not called "The Butler,"—charges hard for the shore. The men are in the back, and note the hydrolic arms for the front plate, the 25mm rapid-firing cannon, and the engine snorkel that allows it to goof around in the surf zone like this without ingesting sea water. Some beach is about to get a visit.

USMC Amtrack

Now because the U.S. Marine Corps is special and different from the U.S. Army (although Marines would just say: "better in every way"), they not only run Bradleys in their operations, but they also have a vehicle that can be deployed from an LCAC off the USS *Tarawa* (the amphibious assault ship) and roll not only onto the beach, but all the way inland as far as you feel like going. This is the AAAV, which stands for "Advanced Amphibious Assault Vehicle," and unfortunately isn't just named the Butler (after Smedley Butler, two-time winner of the Medal of Honor and commandant of the Marine Corps—just a suggestion!). The Butler (oops! I mean the AAAV) shows interesting similarities with, and differences from, the Bradley. It has a driver in the front left and the engine to the right, a gunner to run the 12.7mm machine gun in a turret on the right, and the commander sits behind the driver with his own viewing turret to help him grasp just what is going on. But its hull has a decidedly nautical look to it, with a real bow, and the rear compartment can take up to twenty-five fully-equipped and battle-ready Marines, if in no great comfort or elegance, but Marines have never insisted on that. They just want to be taken far enough forward to commence the whuppin' of whatever enemy unwisely presents themselves.

The AAAV can easily negotiate the surf of most decent beaches, and even has water jet propulsion like modern personal watercraft to shoot itself through the waves and onto the beach. Think of it as a 17,000-kg waverunner with an attitude. The more modern version is the AAV7A1, that comes with a new Cummins engine, smoke generation capabilities, and a nifty new 40mm grenade launcher that can reach out and touch anything within about five hundred feet. There is also a command model without the machine gun, and a combat engineer version that has a great mine-clearing system: it's a rocket that fires a long explosive wire which then detonates and clears a path (coincidentally about the width of an AAV7A1) for the troops to keep pushing forward. The 400hp engine is a brute that needs a lot of maintenance, and the Marines in Iraq report two interesting notes for combat operations: first, that if you don't clear your empty shell casings away they have the ability to find just the right crevice and jam the gun turret; and second, that the military issue lubricant isn't as good as civilian WD-40. Also, as you might expect out of any of these modern armored vehicles, their crew and passengers go through a lot of bottles of water in a day, especially if they're high-tailing it around the Middle East in the middle of the summer. The ground clearance has been raised a little to about eighteen inches, but even so you can't just run this thing over anything you come across—good drivers and commanders with a mature and experienced eye are still needed.

The Stryker

With the end of the Cold War and the feeling that perhaps a gigantic tank battle on the plains of Europe wasn't the most likely scenario for the immediate future of armed conflict, American military planners began to rethink their previously long-held assumptions as to what balance of weight and firepower was the most desirable for the upcoming century. Cleverly, somebody remembered Bedford Forrest and the historical role of the cavalry, and decided that an even faster critter than the Bradley was going to be just the ticket. This process went on for almost fifteen years, but today we are seeing the fruits of those labors in the new Stryker armored vehicle.

One of the endless debates at the armored officer's and NCO clubs has been treads versus tires. The track and tread contingent has always held that nothing but a metallic tread could hope to deal with all the bad places that tanks and fighting vehicles get sent. But with the advent of the run-flat tire and some startling advances in powerplants and weapon systems, what was to become the Stryker began life as the LAV-25 (Light Armored Vehicle). It is a fast little bugger that will almost do 50 mph on a road, and almost that fast when it goes eight-wheel-

The Stryker lighting off its main gun—note the recoil as shown by the dust coming off the tires. This is just one configuration, but the modern cannon is hard-hitting and far-ranged.

ing—because it is indeed an 8x8 system with big tires that are driven by a 275-hp six-cylinder GM diesel.

With a 25mm chain gun in its two-man turret, and the ability to house up to six troops in the back, the Stryker is the obvious evolutionary result of what the Bradley had to teach us (and in fact the standard turret is the same one used on the

The Stryker is the latest U.S. armored vehicle, and the first with wheels since the half-tracks of World War II. It rolls on eight "run flat" tires, and comes in a variety of optional packages, from missile-launching to MedEvac to Command models (which probably have comfy seats). The Stryker Brigade was deployed to Iraq in the fall of 2003, but the results are not in yet. We do know that at least two have tipped over. Easy on the corners, boys! It does 62 mph and can be offloaded from a C130 (above)—someone's predicting a lot more brushfire wars, it seems.

Bradley), and as a result it is faster, and can still be loaded into a C130 and even slung under a rather large helicopter if the need arises. The front four wheels have power-assisted steering for those tight corners that sometimes need to be taken in combat, and it is fully amphibious (at the insistence of the USMC) with bilge pumps and two propellers at the back (or stern, one should say when in the water). This same platform also comes in many different flavors, in case you want a plush ride for the commander of the unit, or a 120mm mortar, or a 90mm gun, or a range of antitank missiles, or a medical suite on wheels that can extract casualties in jig time

Seen here from the rear, where the infantry unloads, the Stryker is the latest round of the "tires versus treads" debate, and seems to be a well-designed and capable addition to the U.S. arsenal.

from the open and dangerous killing grounds and transport them to a safe rear area where they keep the doctors.

Aluminum armor and new construction methods make the Stryker about half the weight of the Bradley, and about one-sixth of what an Abrams clocks in at. All of those factors, plus new doctrine means that not only can this thing get taken to hot spots in one hell of a hurry, but it then has no problem with racing around the battlefield. The Stryker brings back the old head-long spirit of the cavalry of yore, and does so in a thoroughly modern version of the Rolls Royce armored car that first rolled

The welter of feedback that a modern armored vehicle commander has to contend with is well illustrated by this interior view of a Stryker. Data, data, everywhere.

out eighty years ago—but in this case it is better protected and can hit much harder than the somewhat genteel .303 machine guns of those far-off days. How far has the Stryker come since its beginnings? So far that it is now the centerpiece of the Stryker Brigade, a rapid deployment force whose first rapid deployment will be to Iraq this year (2003) to replace the troops who have been overseas for too many months. The initial tests in California and Louisiana were so promising that before the year is out the new Stryker (named for two Medal of Honor winners) will be striking in the desert, and woe betide the Syrian or Iranian vehicle that runs afoul of it. And it will fit in streets where the Abrams could never go, reflecting the best guess as to what the nature of future wars will hold for America's proud armored legions.

CHAPTER 6

Rotors in the Sky: Transport and Combat Helicopters

AFTER AN EXHAUSTIVE look at the history, development, and operations of modern helicopters, you could be forgiven for stating flatly: "There's no way this clattering contraption could work, and even if there was, there's no way a human could fly it." Helicopters are very unlikely beasts, not much like birds, but instead as complicated and finicky as any collection of parts ever assembled, and with the glide characteristics of a brick when the engine fails. And flying them in a combat zone doesn't make them much safer—quite the opposite.

And yet they can and do fly, and intrepid U.S. Army, Air Force, Navy, Marine, and Coast Guard pilots take them up at all hours of the day and night, in all weather, and get where they want to go, and mostly they get back. But far more than simply making it, helicopters have often provided devastating combat firepower, as well as Search & Rescue (SAR), and its violent brother Combat Search & Rescue (CSAR), and every manner of insertion and extraction (as military people call it when they are entering or departing some bad place with troublesome opponents bent on thwarting their desires).

The word "helicopter" comes from the Greeks and is a combination of "heliko" (referring to a spiral) and "pteron"(meaning wing). Leonardo daVinci left us with a drawing of an aerial screw (which may explain why his model was never deployed at full scale). Supposedly the father of the Wright Brothers brought home a top that could be activated by a string and made to fly quite high for a toy, and the brothers evidently enjoyed and experimented with this novelty. Such a toy was the hit of the 1784 World's Fair in Paris, and still today you can see the seed pods of trees spinning gracefully to earth in what must certainly have been an inspiration to early thinkers of mad thoughts about flight.

Sir George Cayley came up with a design in 1843 that isn't that far from the modern Osprey (more on that troubled craft later), in that it had a central fuselage (with a jaunty animal head bow sprit) and arms coming out either side supporting four rotating discs (two per side, mounted atop one another). It was meant to have a steam engine that moved the rotating wheels fast enough to make it go somewhere, but, as with all helicopters, the terrible phrase "highly unstable" kept cropping up. As with most aspects of manned flight, there is considerable debate about who the first person was who got all the strange factors of lift to work out in the sphere of helicopter flight, but the Frenchman Louis Breguet has as good a claim as anyone, and his odd craft did manage to fly—all of two feet off the ground.

The legendary Igor Sikorsky numbered many triumphs of aerial engineering in his long career, including the building of two unsuccessful helicopter models in his native Russia before he came to the United States in 1919. There he focused on fixed wing designs before his amazing breakthrough of 1938. But rotary flight appealed to every visionary thinker of that time, and the amazing Nazi test pilot Hanna Reitsch even demonstrated the new Focke-Achgelis FW-61 by flying it indoors, in the massive Deutschland Hall in Berlin. By then helicopters were developing fast, but they still showed teething pains and retained their "highly unstable" nature, as they have up to the present day.

Fortunately Igor Sikorsky had never forgotten his dreams of helicopter flight, and in 1938 he managed to get his single-rotor VS300 up and off the ground (often flying it himself in his standard test pilot garb of three-piece suit, overcoat, and fedora). And it was the military model of this Sikorsky, the R4, that made some of the first combat excursions during World War II, as well as the first rescues. The helicopter's ability to take off vertically (almost), hover steadily in the sky (more or less, depending on the pilot's skills), and land by descending straight down, meant that a whole new world of military applications and operations were now opened up to the planners of that global conflict, and some even saw a day when entire squads might be airlifted into and out of battle, not to mention the fact that it might now be possible to search for downed pilots or wounded infantrymen on the ground, spot them, descend and snatch them up, and fly away clean.

However, we should stop here and reflect for a moment that the modern training for mountain rescue personel dealing with helicopters has two salient caveats, to wit: 1) If you work with choppers for medical evacuation, that's fine, but make sure you have a back-up plan, because if the pilot gets any lights on his dash he will set it down, and so he should, so it may not be coming; and 2) Everything about helicopters is dangerous, from vectoring them in for a landing where they will blow any loose clothing, gear, or persons off the mountain, to approaching them on the ground (always from the right front where the pilot can

A nice shot of the AH-64D Longbow from the side, showing the in-line seating arrangement for the pilot and the weapons officer.

see you), to loading injured people and then flying out with them. Basically, until the rotor stops turning and you're back on the ground, all bets are off.

But you have to contrast all that with the unparalleled abilities of the chopper as a reconnaissance platform, MedEvac monster, tank killing hawk of the skies, and the fact that nothing else can quite do what a helicopter does. There's an old theatrical and literary expression that comes to mind when you're reading about some of the amazing rescues in Korea and Vietnam and every other conflict since about 1950: *"deus ex machina,"* which means, literally, "god from the machine." In the early theater, if a playwright was stuck for what would happen

next he could always lower in some deity from an off-stage "machine," just in time for a dramatic rescue. The modern helicopter, and especially the modern combat helicopter, has all the trappings of a classic *deus ex machina*, and has proven that with enough maintenance help and forward operating areas, helicopters can in many ways dominate a battlefield, allowing nothing to happen that you as the commander do not wish to have happen.

The first helicopter war was Vietnam, and while the outcome left much to be desired, the new Air Assault Divisions (starting with the 11th AAD) showed that they could respond quickly to the often sudden combat developments and stealthy maneuvers of a wily guerrilla foe, and not only land hundreds of men in jig time, but also extract them just as quickly. But at a price. The first helicopter deployed to that unhappy land, the slow and banana-shaped CH-21, was only vulnerable to ground fire during a few moments of its flight; unfortunately those moments included the approach, the landing, the unloading, and the subsequent takeoff. It should be expected that any enemy will be clever and desperate enough to find ways to neutralize technological advantages, and the Viet Cong were among the most fervent at this. Early helicopter operations were often bungled terribly due to inadequate firepower and an enemy who knew how to slay these dragons from the sky that brought our troops and one hundred kinds of death to their country.

Interestingly, after some departmental head-butting, the U.S. Army became the lead player in chopper operations. The training ground became Fort Rucker, Alabama, and legend has it that early rotary aviators were started out flying with an instructor who would go over what the various controls were supposed to do, and then fly the student to a 40-acre field. The first task was to try to hover, and keep it in that field. This sounds simple if you've never grappled with a collective and a cyclic and rudder pedals. Once the pilot starts responding a little late, and putting in too much control thus overcontrolling the craft, he hasn't got a prayer of staying in that field, and general aviation in Mississippi should be on the lookout for him as well.

Flying helicopters is as simple as riding a bike while juggling three balls and reciting Shakespeare. Then have a friend throw rocks at you and you'll have the tiniest inkling of what a chore it is to get the machine to do what you want it to do in a military setting. The controls are the familiar joy stick (called the cyclic in this case) in your right hand, the collective pitch control in your left hand, and your feet on the rudder pedals that control the amount of movement and direction of the tail rotor. To hover keep the rotor level (with the cyclic) and feed in pitch (changing the angle of attack of the spinning blades) with the collective until lift overcomes weight and up she goes … oh, and to keep it from mimicking a Waring blender, you'll need a fair amount of left pedal until you're out of "ground effect" (where the air generated by the rotors splashes off the ground and helps to propel you up).

Now you and it will be free to move in three dimensions … and your vehicle will seemingly have a mind of its own, so just keep balancing the collective and the cyclic and the rudders to keep it absolutely still … or not. Soon you can try to go somewhere, and this involves tilting the rotors (using the swash plate hooked to your cyclic) forward, which should impart forward flight, and then you'll gain some speed and slowly pull up on the collective while twisting it (like a motorcycle throttle) to add pitch until you are able to climb up and away. To simply take off straight up requires more power than many choppers can muster, so you always try to get a running start if you can. In Vietnam this sometimes meant hovering forward to the edge of some handy cliff and then hoping that when the ground drops away you will do the same until a safe flying speed is achieved. You find that sometimes it's best if your passengers are preoccupied with their own affairs while you do this.

All these dang systems affect each other, so if you pull too much collective on your takeoff, you'll have to work everything else like a one-arm paper hanger, and your problems can escalate from there to the point where you're a steaming mass of twisted, smoking rubble on the ground. To avoid this, pilots have extraordinary training after they have shown they have extraordinary skills, and a few tricks up their flight suit sleeves, such as "autorotation." Autorotation is the amazing ability of a chopper with a dead motor to land if the pilot is very cool headed and does everything just right—which involves putting the nose down and diving for the ground when the engine quits, and then yanking the bird back into a flared landing at just the right moment. It may wreck your ride home, but you (and your passengers) won't wind up busticated … maybe. Basically, you are using the forward speed to make the rotors turn enough to impart some semblance of lift to the vehicle, much as the old autogyros did, and then gambling that this will be enough to cushion your fall from the sky if you flare at the right moment.

The amazing pilots in Vietnam did all of these things and more, and often did them under withering fire from the ground, risking everything to drop troops off or pick them up, and most of all to recover downed pilots. There were Distinguished Flying Crosses and Silver Stars handed out left and right, and a couple of Medals of Honor, and like all bravery citations these make for astounding reading. How they kept those birds in the air is beyond knowing.

It was during this time that a famous chopper made its name in American military history: the UH-1B, known in every corner of the globe as the Huey. The mighty Huey was a pretty big bird, and it didn't take too many shots from the ground before Hueys were showing up with rockets and machine guns wherever they could be bolted or bungied onto the frame. The Huey became in many ways the symbol of the American involvement in Vietnam, and that's too bad because the war divided the nation as nothing else had since the Civil War. In 1975 it was a Huey that made the last run to the roof of the embassy in Saigon, and footage of pilots crashing them in the ocean after jumping clear near a ship, or men pushing them over the side of aircraft carriers to make room for the next overloaded flight, were indelibly seared into many brains.

128

The Huey would serve for many, many years, and they are still out there flying for the National Guard and U.S. Army Reserve units. But Cyrus Vance, then secretary of the army, decided that what was needed was an entirely new attack helicopter, and this contract eventually went to Lockheed, who produced the AH-56 Cheyenne in May of 1967. The Cheyenne is a very thin chopper with a pilot and copilot seated one ahead of the other, and its purpose was to fly into danger and blast the living daylights out of whatever threat it could find and nail. The Cheyenne had two little wings that acted as airfoils when it exceeded one hundred knots, as well as making a handy attachment point for rockets and miniguns. Flat out it would do 256 mph, and that made it a very fast-moving response to trouble in Vietnam. The Lockheed Cheyenne suffered from convoluted complexity and a number of mechanical oddities that never could be ironed out, and as a result it lost the confidence of the politicians as well as the flyers, and was cancelled in 1972.

Bell Helicopters had an even better idea, and they were quicker at understanding the situation in Vietnam and responding in a way that pleased the men on the front lines. The result of this was the AH-1G Huey Cobra, using as many parts of the old Huey as possible, which became known to the Viet Cong as "Whispering Death" for its quiet motor and pointedly hostile capabilities.

But the idea of Air Cavalry had reached a state where not only could masses of troops be air assaulted into a combat area, but they also had their own little scouts (the "Loach") zipping around looking for trouble, and the Huey Cobra for when something needed to be blasted off the face of the earth. It's interesting to note that the ancient and archaic idea of cavalry (well, at least until Special Forces took to the saddle in Afghanistan in 2001!) traveled two roads to the modern day, one through

Above a Huey offloads men in Vietnam at a spot where landing would be dangerous—almost as dangerous as jumping off those skids six feet up. Many broken and sprained legs and ankles resulted from this maneuver, but it allowed us to insert men in unexpected places during Vietnam, the first helicopter war.

Today the Huey is still used in training. Here a U.S. Marine demonstrates one way to get to the ground quickly. He is wearing a harness, and his right hand controls the rate of descent down the rope—quickly to start, then hopefully slower as the ground gets closer. Experienced rappellers can get to the ground very fast using this method.

An AH-64 Apache skims along at low level. Apaches can lurk behind a stand of trees and pop up to fire off their missiles, and just as easily go tearing along at ground level to get from place to place quickly, relying on the pilot's nerve and training to stay clear of the hard earth.

armored vehicles and the other through helicopters. Jeb Stuart would have been torn, but helicopters probably would have appealed to his free-ranging concept of just what it means to take a "look see."

Vietnam saw some clever ways of defeating helicopters as well, such as stringing wires in areas where choppers were expected. The savage Viet Cong also would sometimes wait for the last chopper to land and disgorge troops, and then shoot it down, drawing in FACs and rescue choppers, while separate troops attacked the Americans who were now without a ride home, and in a world of trouble. Despite all this, the American pilots in Vietnam (and their Air America counterparts "over the fence" in Cambodia and Laos) blazed some bright trails to glory as they brought an exceptional mobility to warfare on a scale never before seen.

However, learning how to jink around the mountains and rice paddies of Southeast Asia was not the same as what appeared to be the next dust-up on the horizon, and that was the possibility that an endless stream of cheaply made and sturdy Soviet tanks would just pour through Germany and enslave all of Europe. To address this, the Ansbach trials were run during April and May of 1972 using Canadian and German participants as well as Americans, and it was found that the tactics used in Vietnam were no longer the right answer. The new god was "Nap of the Earth," and remains in power to this day. This means that you need to run your rig close to the ground, pop up and engage targets, and duck back into the trees like a kid playing dodge ball—otherwise you'd be blown out of the sky. The direct result of this exercise was a revamping of the training American combat helicopter pilots received, and the impetus for a new platform: The Apache. Oh, there's still Huey Cobras out there bringing "whispering death" to old enemies and new, but the Apache is the new kid on the block, and it's quite the little sky car when the shooting starts.

The AH-64A Apache helicopter is the one we're using right now, and it's 58.3 feet long with the rotors, a svelte 16.3 feet wide out to the end of the weapon pod winglets, 12.7 feet tall, and weighs 10.5 tons. The Apache has proven to be a complicated platform to keep in the air, but it's ten tons of death that can take advanced weaponry three hundred miles at 227 mph, and that's not to be sniffed at. It's a tank killer supreme, and can pop

An AH-64D Longbow. This picture shows the sensor pod above the rotors, as well as the chain gun below the nose that is linked to the helmet of the fliers. Where they look, it points—in this case, straight ahead.

up, fire off its Hellfire missiles in a salvo, and duck back down like a jack in the box. Most often, the enemy can't hit what it can't see. Two men fly this thing, a pilot and a gunner, and the gunner controls the missiles and rockets, as well as the 30mm chain gun under the nose, which is linked to his helmet so he just has to look at something and touch the trigger to have it vaporized. It can be flown in the dark as well as in the light, and through weather that would drown a duck. With advanced target acquisition designation sights, the pilot's night-vision system, infrared countermeasures and nap of the earth navigation at high speeds, this is one heck of a package, even if the mechanics do grumble about it. But after all, they spend two hours fixing it for every one hour of flight, and that would make anyone bitter.

A total of 530 Apaches have been upgraded to the AH-64D, which can hang sixteen Hellfires off its wings, and has advanced digital avionics and a funny looking pod on top of the rotor, know by the ancient name "Longbow." This turns the average Apache into a device that cannot only sense and target the enemy, but also transmit and coordinate attacks between a range of different options, including A-10 Warthogs and the "fast movers," the jets of the U.S. Navy and Air Force.

The modern Huey transport (or "slick" as they were called in Vietnam) is the UH-60 Blackhawk. We have better than one thousand of them, and they are massive and reliable craft— well, as reliable as a chopper ever gets. They won't survive being shot at too much, as we found out to our chagrin in Somalia, but as a state of the art people mover, they have no equal.

When we really had to move a lot of people in the old days we deployed the venerable CH-47 Chinook, a twin-rotor monster that could carry fifty-six men and their gear quite a long way, and up to 15,000 feet (unique among helicopters, which also

This is just what you don't want to see in your rearview mirror if you're driving an enemy tank. The Apache is our tank-killer supreme, and when they tilt over like this they are cleared to fire off those sixteen antitank missiles on the stubby wing pods, or deploy the chain gun under the nose. Pilots are split as to whether this maneuver is called "crank and bank" or "turn and burn." Notice the two engines and the sensor pod above the rotor, making this a "Longbow."

The forward tilt in this picture indicates that this UH-60 Blackhawk is picking up speed and going forward at a good clip. These helicopters are the troop-carrying workhorses of the modern U.S. chopper fleet, but they can be brought down by an enemy with enough RPGs—as proved in Somalia.

made the Chinook a spanking fine answer to mountainous CSAR (Combat Search and Rescue). And today's Chinook, the Improved Cargo Helicopter (ICH) is the same old updated CH-47F, but now with two .50-caliber machine guns, and the option of hanging a Stinger missile off the stubby wings. And if you think one rotor is hard to fly, try two of them counter rotating.

For Special Forces and other strange and dangerous jobs, the best answer is the MH-53 Pave Low, which is a huge helicopter (eighty-eight feet long with rotor, twenty-five feet high) with

The Blackhawk is our modern Huey, an all-purpose carrier that can get troops on the battlefield quickly. But helicopters are never more vulnerable than when they are on the ground or hovering nearby, so the unloading is typically a very rapid evolution. The sensors on their helmets and yellow boxes on the muzzles of the M16s indicate that this is a wargame. And look at those packs! These guys intend to be on the ground for a while.

The mighty Chinook doing some cargo work in Vietnam. Although they are aging rapidly, the CH-47 is just too good a design to let go, sort of like the B-52 and M113. The Chinook's heavy-cargo carrying ability, and its versatility in mountainous terrain made it the work-horse of choice in Vietnam.

massive engines that can drive it for six hundred miles at 165 mph. It carries six crew: two pilots, two flight engineers, and two door gunners (one for each side, or they can fight over who gets to shoot out of the back hatch when the ramp is down in flight). In emergencies they can take this bird and jam 50,000 pounds aboard it, and the two GE T64-GE/100 engines will still allow it to leave the ground.

The U.S. Navy uses the venerable Sea King, the Sikorsky SH-3D, for most of its offshore work. The Sea King is much beloved among naval pilots for its ability to operate in dreadful conditions, which may be every day for a week if you're operat-

Two Chinooks using their massive lift capability to sling-load two Humvees in Alaska. Note the skis on the wheels, and the unique twin counter-rotating props.

ing out of sight of land, and for its huge capacity for crew, passengers, and cargo. Its brother, the SH-60 Seahawk, is used for antisubmarine patrols, using sophisticated sensors and towed buoys to spot and then dispatch enemy subs with an air-dropped torpedo. The Seahawk also doubles as the cargo carrier and Special Operations choice of the U.S. Navy, and has done very well in its role wearing many hats.

Also in the Special Operations world is the 160th SOAR (Special Operations Aviation Regiment), the "Nightstalkers."

They claim "We own the night," and as it turns out they're right about that. With night-vision helmets and goggles and a full range of avionic sensors, the 160th deploys MH-6 and AH-6 "Little Birds" for a quick look at things, and then the MH-60 and AH-60 when they need to get larger, all the way up to the MH-47E Chinook, which comes with miniguns that can spit out 6,000 rounds a minute.

In modern wars, such as the recent liberation of Afghanistan, the USAF would provide AC-130s and A-10s to

The Navy's all-weather Search & Rescue (SAR) platform, the SH-60 Seahawk, is seen here with the starboard door open and a diver being recovered by a sling and hoist as the pilot hovers over a windswept sea. If you're a jet jockey who has gone down in the drink, this is what you want to see coming to you.

protect the helicopters, and then fly the troops in on the UH/EH-60A Blackhawk and the MH-47 Chinook, although it is an older craft and very sensitive about things like having shots bounce off it. And if there's some further problem, the Army has its own AH-64 Apaches standing by to tear things up but good.

But you must not forget the great complexity of these machines, or the massive effort it takes to field them when America goes to war. An excellent base is needed with unlimited fuel and really patient mechanics just to get the fancy rigs close

The OH-6 made its debut in Vietnam, where it was used as a command and control platform for other helicopters and troops on the ground. Today it is used in both those roles, as well as having the capability to be heavily armed and work with U.S. Special Forces. Very small and agile, the OH-6 is perfect for urban warfare, such as in Panama, where it helped Delta Force liberate prisoners in town.

to where the pilots can show off some of their peerless skills by doing all the great things choppers do, such as peek over the next hill, line up and destroy targets that are appropriate to them (such as tanks and trucks), land the Special Forces and then the Air Assault troops (such as the 101st "Screaming Eagles"), and pop in at just the right moment to extract either men who need to leave all their troubles behind, or those in need of medical atten-

A thirsty MH-53 Pave Low IV creeps up on the refueling nozzle of a MC-130P Combat Shadow to prevent being out of fuel—"Bingo." This one is from the 21st Special Operations Squadron, and these are all-weather, day-and-night helicopters of a massive size and extraordinary capability—matched only by their pilots.

tion. The helicopter is a wondrous invention, adept at unusual and unique maneuvers that would overtask any airplane or ground vehicle, and yet … that phrase "dangerously unstable" keeps coming up. The Coast Guard does use an "auto hover" device that takes a little of the danger out of operation at night over a raging sea in zero visibility. But still, although there are pilots who can control these things, and do so amazingly well in combat and under conditions that would make you and I ill just to watch in a movie, the chopper will always be a triumph of engineering that is very, very dangerous to its users.

CHAPTER 7

Death from Above: U.S. Military Air Power

NAPOLEON'S MILITARY MAXIMS go on for many, many pages, as one might expect of one of the greatest and most studied of all generals. Oddly, they don't include the helpful hints: "Don't invade Russia," or "When they put you on an island under guard, stay there." But even taking into account the convoluted nature of nineteenth-century discourse, and the perils of translation, one precept comes up time and again: "Take the high ground." It sounds a lot more elegant in French, but it's easy to grasp the wisdom of this admonition in the realm of military matters. The various hills, ridges, and mountains of the world have always been sought out as strongholds that can defy attacks, while also improving your ability to see the enemy coming.

But if you really want to solidify your position, today you've got to take it upstairs. Once the reckless Montgolfier brothers of France had perfected their balloons, it didn't take long for the army guys to see the utility of this gasbag, and balloons were soon floating over many prominent battlefields, and being shot at by disgruntled ground pounders. Balloons have pretty serious limitations, such as the fact that they are often at the mercy of the winds. But with the development of manned powered flight by the Wright brothers on a windy day at Kitty Hawk, North Carolina, on December 17, 1903, (or the French, British, Russian, Prussian, and Australian contenders—pretty much everybody except Mr. Langley of the Smithsonian!) it wasn't more than a decade before the world embraced the notion of aerial combat and reconnaissance. Mankind evidently has some deep-seated need to turn everything to warfare eventually, and flight was just too useful to remain in the pacifist camp for long.

World War I saw these motorized kites evolve very quickly into semi-reliable platforms that could mount guns and provide not only intelligence from the front lines, but even drop bombs and strafe the infantry, adding just another layer of misery to what was already a most disagreeable war. It wasn't long before the Americans got involved, first with the legendary volunteers of the Lafayette Escadrille (young Yanks who flew for France before our entry into the war), and then with an Army Air Corps that got up to speed quickly and was blessed with such hotheaded and visionary pilots and commanders as Eddie Rickenbacker (America's leading ace), Arizona balloon-buster Frank Luke, and Billy Mitchell, the prophet of air power, whose lack of diplomatic skills ensured that nobody had the slightest inclination to listen to his very good points about the decisive effects of bombing ships and troops.

Between the wars, men like Jimmy Doolittle proved that not only could American pilots fly with the best the world had to offer, but in Doolittle's case, they could also attend MIT and make the first landing on instruments alone. The combination of cerebral acumen and daredevil flying was firmly in place, and

A B-17 "Flying Fortress," the best American bomber of World War II, is shown having dropped its load on what looks like an enemy airbase (note the runway to the left of the bomb smoke). These huge and heavily armed bombers were the backbone of the "Mighty Eighth" U.S. Army Air Corps in its effort to bomb the Germans into submission—at which it failed, despite the bravery and losses of the aircrews.

has continued to this day. Not only that, but a certain style was developed that included lengthy descriptions of flight involving much hand gesturing (just go to any small airport and watch for this even today), and an entire line of fashion, typified by the wearing of lace-up high boots (which are actually not that helpful on the rudder pedals), jodhpurs, and the ubiquitous flight jacket. Pilots to this day would sooner walk than give up their leather jackets.

World War II saw the overwhelming dominance of American air power, as such amazing planes as the B-17 "Flying Fortress" long-range bomber made their appearance, along with the

P-38 twin-tail attack aircraft (the "Lightning"), and the P-47 "Thunderbolt." But it was the P-51 "Mustang" that pointed the way to the future. This wonderful fighter had a massive piston engine up front, and combined the range needed to accompany the bombers on their way to the German heartland with the firepower to wreck anything they found among the clouds. Funny what eight .50-caliber M2 machine guns will do. In the Pacific, airplanes like the Corsair and the B-26 chewed up the Japanese Zeros most effectively, and of course the aerial dropping of the atomic bomb put an end to the grim specter of an invasion of the home islands.

But it should be noted that while there was ample evidence of the effectiveness of air power as an adjunct to combined arms operations, such as when the skies cleared in December of 1944 the desperate German thrust known as "the battle of the Bulge" came to a grinding halt, air power alone was not enough to win wars. This topic has been the main bone of contention in many, many debates, most of them involving budgetary matters. Basically, the U.S. Air Force (as it became known after 1947) wanted to have some of the oceanic budget of the U.S. Navy, and neither side has ever been willing to back down from their contention that their branch of the service is in reality the essential one.

Be that as it may, the Cold War brought us into an era of "mutually assured destruction," a sort of "Mexican stand off" where neither the United States nor the Russians or Chinese would be able to whack the other guy and walk away clean. By the 1950s there were enough long-range bombers and missiles to pretty much guarantee that any nuclear head-butting would set off a cataclysm that would reduce the world (and its competing economic systems) to a frangible cinder floating through space. This awful possibility may well have prevented such an occurrence.

Meanwhile, the fighter jocks just wanted to know when the

next Dawn Patrol was scheduled. There was a fair amount of aerial scrimmaging in the skies of Korea during our "police action" there (which cost us fifty thousand good men), and the Chinese pilots and their Russian Migs proved to make great targets for the new American jets. By that time the old piston engines had gone about as fast as they could go, which was damn fast (close to 500 mph), and the jet age was upon us. Today's turbojets are astounding machines, which can not only thrust an airplane through the sky so fast you can barely see it, but also require extensive maintenance. Basically, jet engines take air in the front and pressurize it, before injecting fuel and igniting the mixture, and the result is one hell of a blast of air coming out the back of the engine. There's also the afterburner at the tail end, which uses the exhaust to combine with more fuel to get an even bigger push. This allows jets to do things like fly at Mach 2.5 (in the case of the F-15), fly straight up into the sky (this doesn't work so well with a piston engine and a propeller), and scream around combat zones like Valkyries gone mad. But keep in mind that any aircraft can be stalled at any time—just arrange it so there isn't enough wind coming over the wings, and that annoying stall horn will start its caterwauling.

Flight is inherently dangerous, much the same as naval operations. There are no "routine flights," despite what people would have you believe. Small airplanes crash with depressing regularity, and not a few airliners have gone down over the years. Flying is still safer than driving (which ought to cross your mind as you drive to the hardware store blasting the radio and thinking about everything except your driving), but any time you leave the ground, and especially if you do so with the intent of waging war, there will always be an element of danger. Fighter pilots actually like this feature of their chosen profession, which is just one reason why they are fighter pilots and we are not.

In Vietnam, the United States tried time and again to get

anybody to agree that we were winning, because we certainly pounded the snot out of that country using every weapon we could lay our hands on, not the least air power. General Curtis Lemay of the U.S. Air Force has the unfortunate distinction of having claimed that we would be able to "bomb them back into the stone age," but at the end of those fifteen years it was our side that looked a little troglodytic, and we had 58,000 fewer men to debate the "domino theory." It proved to be all but impossible to win that war using air strikes alone, although the Vietnamese casualties were in the millions, and this despite our wonderful airplanes and pilots, not to mention some of the most devastating bombing strikes the world has ever seen. When the mighty B-52s let loose their loads on a quiet patch of jungle, the swath was often a mile wide and five miles long.

But the United States military cannot be blamed for what was essentially a political mistake in the pursuit of global objectives, and during those years the USAF had been honing their skills, along with the Navy and USMC pilots, to the extent that much of our modern air power thinking comes directly out of this period. Today's pilots and planes are better than they have ever been, and it's a little hard to see who could seriously take off and give any of our jets a problem. Fighter-to-fighter encounters remain in many ways the same as they were in 1914 when the first unfriendly soul took a potshot at his opposite number, in that surprise accounts for almost all fighter successes. If you can see the other guy first, you can usually nail him. It just happens a lot more quickly today. The best place to attack is still from the rear, either above or below, and diving out of the sun never goes out of style.

But there are a great many tasks for a modern air force that don't include trying to shoot down an enemy with a silk scarf and a bad attitude. Air power means being able to detect and thwart

your enemy's intentions, and it also includes striking ground targets and moving masses of troops and gear across several time
zones at a moment's notice. This, as you might expect, is a big job.
Today's United States Air Force is a fantastically complicated enti-
ty that can deploy everything from Fuel Air Explosives and "smart
bombs" to their own Special Forces, including Pathfinders to set up
and run remote landing strips, and the PJs (Pararescue Jumpers),
medically savvy commandos who are called in for CSAR (Combat
Search & Rescue). The USAF is the mightiest air force the world has
ever seen, and the full range of their weaponry makes for a staggering inventory.

The Planes

Out in front is the F/A-18 Hornet. Looking at it from the nose,
what you'll see is a slender dart with two engines on either side
of the fuselage. Those are General Electric F-404-400 augmented
turbofans, and they'll put out 16,000 pounds of thrust each when
you turn the key. This fighter is the most versatile and deadly of
our many jets, and it can fly in a straight line about 2,000 miles,
although its combat radius is more like 425 nautical miles, allowing for travel time and combat, with a reserve (called "Bingo" by
fighter pilots, meaning "just enough gas to get home"). It's fifty-
six feet long and forty feet wide from wing tip to wing tip, and
you can hang so much crap (in the form of bombs, rockets, and
missiles) on this plane that when fully loaded the standard fighter attack weight of 34,000 pounds goes right on up to almost
50,000 pounds. The Hornet comes in single-seat and two-seat
models, and at top speed it can propel those guys at Mach 1.8,
which is about 1,188 mph. The McDonnell Douglas Corporation
has taken some heat for the cost overruns and performance
shortcomings of this fighter, but the various kinks have been

The pride of naval aviation, this is the mighty F/A-18E Super Hornet, seen here geared up for whatever trouble may lurk. It's carrying two 2,000-lb. bombs, two AGM-88 High Speed Anti-Radiation (HARM) missiles, and two AIM-9 Sidewinders, so it can destroy enemy radar, other jets, or any target on the ground.

honed and smoothed to the point where this all-weather attack and bombing jet is one of the most feared aerial weapons platforms in the world.

In the nose of this plane is an M61 multi-barrel 20mm cannon with 540 rounds waiting to spool out so quickly you can be out of ammunition in a heartbeat. Fighter pilots call this condition "Winchester," a generic term meaning "I'm all out of rocks to throw at the bad guys." But to get the Hornet to Winchester takes some doing, as it can carry a staggering load of 17,000 lbs. worth of assorted falling doom, in the form of nine stations along the wings and body where all manner of rockets and missiles can be hung, and released by the handy toggle switch on the joy stick. These include the anti-ship Harpoon missile, as well as air-to-air Sidewinders and AIM-7s. There are various places to put pods like the one that contains the FLIR (forward looking

infrared radar), the all-weather sensor that enables them to see the other guy before he sees them.

Hornets are operated by the USAF, the U.S. Navy, and the U.S. Marine Corps, and are equally happy landing on carriers as they are on remote airstrips. They can be throttled down to a mere 131 knots for putting it down on a flat top, and that's mighty slow for a modern jet. One guesses from that figure that the stall speed is about 125 knots. Landing on carriers has been likened to parking a car at 100 miles an hour, and indeed there are few things as terrifying to civilians as the notion of trying to land on a little speck (all 1,100 feet of a Nimitz-class carrier) in the middle of the vast ocean. But naval fighter pilots have a unique and characteristic contempt for the obvious impossibility of their calling, and a few of them remember Jimmy Doolittle using B-24 bombers flown off a carrier to attack Japan a few months after

Pearl Harbor. As pilots say: "Take off is optional; landing is mandatory." And for this, naval aviators train long and hard to bring their F/A-18s and F-14s onto and off aircraft carriers. There can be no doubt that it takes a very special individual to pilot a Hornet that is first thrown bodily off the front of the flight deck. He flies somewhere and bombs something, and then has to nurse his multi-ton jet back onto the correct glide slope to arrive back at the arresting wires strung across the after deck before he can go below and get some food and rest before the next mission.

Grumman Aerospace makes the F-14 Tomcat, which is the heavier brother of the F/A-18, and is primarily a carrier-based fighter-bomber. The F-14 is a massive aircraft with twin tails and wings that can be swept either forward for slow flight or aft when you wish to hit the afterburner and leave some unfortunate incident in your wake. It's all of sixty-five feet long, and the wings can be put out to sixty-four feet, or swept back to a mere thirty-eight feet. A pair of Pratt & Whitney TF-30-414 turbofans makes it go to the tune of Mach 2.4, which is about 1,600 mph. Both the F-14 and the F/A-18 have a service ceiling of over 50,000 feet, and they can use this ability to loiter far above their carrier group, ready to swoop down and pounce on any threat to their ride home. With nothing on it for weapons the Tomcat weighs twenty tons, but if they've got a job to do the maximum weight is an awesome 74,348 pounds. Fully loaded the Tomcat weighs about what a German Tiger tank weighed, and it's hard to imagine launching one of those off the front of a carrier—for a very brief flight. But unlike the Tiger, when the Tomcat gets up and running it can do close to 900 mph at sea level (the Mach 2.4 is for high-altitude work), and when it's armed with its full panoply, it has a range of deadly options. This would include the standard M61 Vulcan cannon with 675 rounds in 20mm, as well as four AIM-7 Sparrow AAMs (air-to-air missiles), and the Sidewinders and Phoenix missiles, so that

The Navy's swept-wing F-14 Tomcat is seen here "pickling" off a GBU-24B/B hard target Penetrator laser-guided bomb which can be vectored into an open window by Special Forces on the ground—an amazing advance in attacking hardened bunkers.

there isn't any target they have to pass up, muttering into their headset: "If I'd only brought a ..."

The swept wing is a very clever idea, as it gives you two airplanes for the price of one. The computer controls the angle of the wing, and as a result you can sweep them all the way back if you wish to go very damn fast and maneuver like a bee-stung mule, or extend them almost straight out when you need to get back to the carrier and more lift is needed. The Tomcat can take off in less than one thousand feet (with the catapult kicking it in the ass) and land in under two thousand feet (using the arresting wires), and for a massive jet that can carry almost 15,000 pounds of bombs and missiles, that's pretty amazing. Two guys get to ride this puppy around, a pilot and a navigator, and the evidence suggests that there's more than enough for the two of them to do, even with modern computers aiding their flight, and the Honeywell laser-gyro inertial navigation system humming away.

But when the U.S. military doesn't need to use a $4 billion carrier to move their planes around, they turn to the best land-based fighter ever built. That would be the F-16 Fighting Falcon made by General Dynamics. They have either a Pratt & Whitney or a GE engine, both turbofans, and they'll give about 24,000 pounds of thrust, making for a top speed of 1,350 mph (Mach 2.05), although they have to be at 40,000 feet or above to scoot around that quickly. Down "on the deck" (as low flight is called) they'll still do a respectable 900 mph, and that's fast enough so the other team won't even hear them coming. The F-16 went through a lengthy development stage, and as a result it is the best fighter in the world today, with a straight-line range of 2,400 miles and a tactical range of 340 miles. The idea with a tactical range is that you get to where the whuppin' needs doing as economically as possible, open up the throttle and zip around like a crazed banshee, and then cruise home slowly, watching the gas gauge.

Two USAF F-16 Fighting Falcons looking for trouble, and carrying a full combat load, including the AIM-120 Advanced Medium-Range air-to-air missiles, drop tanks of fuel, and an electronic jamming pod to mess up enemy radar.

The F-16 has a GE M61A-1 20mm cannon in the nose, and can then carry a 2,200-lb. bomb along the fuselage, with inboard and middle wing stations for hanging 3,500-lb. bombs, as well as the AIM-7 Sparrow missile or the Hughes AIM-120 Advanced Medium-Range AIM. Composite materials have reduced the weight of this aircraft to a very small number (15,000 pounds empty), but then you can hang another 20,000 pounds of "BOOM!" on it, and it's as quick as the devil in dogfighting and maneuvering. At a mere forty-seven feet long, and with a wingspan of thirty-one feet, the F-16 almost doesn't look as if it has grown up enough to go into war-troubled skies, but it is more than efficient—the F-16 is absolutely deadly. The nose holds an APG-66 multimode intercept radar, and the HUD (heads-up display) on the cockpit glass shows everything you need to know to find the bad guys and trash them. Instead of the traditional joystick, there is a side-mounted stick, and the whole thing is rigged as a "fly by wire" aircraft, meaning that the computer is doing the actual controlling, with the pilot indicating his or her preferences.

At the other end of the spectrum is the A-10 Thunderbolt (which everybody calls "The Warthog" in a tribute to its graceless looks). When the United States thought that the next war would feature about a million Russian tanks pouring through the Fulda Gap in Europe, the call went out for something that could whack these clanking behemoths from the air, and the answer was the A-10. The Warthog is basically an airplane built around a gun, that gun being the GAU-8/A Avenger 30mm seven-barrel cannon with 1,174 rounds of depleted uranium munitions that can chew the tar out of any vehicle we are likely to find on the planet. The pilot sits in a heavily armored bucket to keep his soft pink parts safe from ground fire, and two enormous GE TF34-100 turbofans are hung on the tail, giving 18,000 lbs. of thrust between them. Empty it weighs 21,519 pounds with a maximum weight up to an incredible 50,000 pounds. The twin tail booms and fuselage serve to hide some of the heat signature of the A-10 to prevent the other team from nicking it with shoulder-launched missiles, an important consideration because the Warthog will only do 423 mph going flat out and downhill. But what it lacks in speed it more than makes up for in maneuverability and firepower. The A-10 is the first choice for columns of enemy trucks, as well as most any armored fight-

An excellent shot of two A-10 Warthogs in close formation, showing off the massive engines, television-guided munitions, and the Gatling gun under the nose. These highly maneuverable tank killers are meant to go in low and slow (relatively) and use their pilot's initiative and guts to blast ground targets, which always gets the thumbs up from the infantry.

The Harrier "jump jet" is seen here hovering placidly over slot number 8 of an amphibious assault ship, showing its capability of landing vertically. You can see the engine thruster angled downward to direct the flow of air that allows them to hover. Tricky and dangerous to fly, the Harrier is nonetheless one of the most versatile and tactical close-air support jets in the world.

ing vehicle in any of the world's armories. It can jink and dive and climb like a kestrel on speed, and if it gets a target it can destroy it with the forward gun so fast that all you'll see is metal flying and an explosion after a bit. If only it could land like a helicopter …

For that you'll need an AV-8B Harrier II, the jump jet developed by the British and now made by McDonnell-Douglas. This astounding airplane can take off and land by pivoting its jet engines and using the thrust to ascend or go down at will, although it takes off better using a ramp (hence the term "jump jet"). The Harrier is a neat idea, a 13,000-pound, single-seat jet that has a Rolls Royce Pegasus 11 turbofan rated for 21,180 pounds of thrust, and clever nozzles that can be directed by the pilot to do what he wishes, from hovering very still to going at 580 knots flat out. It has a GAU-12/U five-barrel Gatling-type cannon in 25mm, and can also carry 9,000 pounds of missiles and bombs. Best of all, at the end of the day the Harrier can simply find a safe place (with fuel and mechanics) and hover down to a steady landing by coming straight down. But all this is not accomplished without a high price: the Harrier is known to be difficult to master, and all too willing to kill student pilots. The USMC uses the Harrier to support its troops in the field, as it has used airplanes since the 1920s in Nicaragua. For some reason Marines wish to have other Marines providing them with air cover and support, and the close-in bravery of their pilots seems to back up their reasoning.

Over on the spooky dark side of modern U.S. military aviation are the deadly Stealth fighters, which were no more than rumors for several years. The rumors proved to be true. The Northrop-Grumman B-2A Spirit is a weird flying wing that costs a mere $21 billion per unit, and that MSRP has been going up over the years since it was first rolled out. Things like a reported

A B-2A Spirit, the bomber version of the new Stealth aircraft, is shown here gently cruising, belying its ability to penetrate any radar system anywhere in the world and dump a hangar full of bombs, rockets, and missiles on previously denied targets. Basically it's a flying wing, and a "fly by wire" platform (where the computer helps you after you tell it what you want to do) that represents a quantum leap in technology.

"electrogravitronic" system of using magnetic fields and smooth surfaces to shield the plane from radar are still highly classified, but we do know that it's almost impossible to detect this plane, and that's too bad for the enemy as it can carry a reported eighty 500-lb. bombs internally and unleash them many miles from its home base.

Then there's the Lockheed-Martin F-117A Nighthawk. This single-seat attack aircraft uses two GE F404-F1D2 engines to power it up to Mach One (about 717 mph), and instead of being

The F-117A Nighthawk. Was it designed at the Bizarro Skunk Works? Yup! All those angles are meant to make it next to impossible for enemy radar to see this fighter-bomber version of Stealth technology coming—until the bombs start dropping. We've come a long way from the old "stick and rudder" days of flight, and with the computer assisting, you evidently can't fly this by the seat of your pants. But something tells us Lt. Frank Luke would have liked it.

all-rounded, has the sharpest and strangest angles of any jet aloft today. It's 65 feet long and 43 feet wide, and there's no way to see it on radar as it comes in. The Nighthawk is an all-weather jet that can carry laser-guided bombs and a range of missiles, and evidently they have done outstanding work in the most recent go-round in Iraq.

Then sometimes they've got to move stuff, and for that the C-5 Galaxy and the C-117 Globemaster are the heavy lifters, while the C-130 Hercules by Lockheed is an old favorite that just won't

The C-130 Hercules is famed around the world for its ability to carry quite a load and land on cruddy short strips in bad weather. Note the massive tail and four huge propeller-driven engines—it handles well, has lots of power, and can maneuver smoothly as a result of its beloved design.

go away. There's a good case to be made for "if it ain't broke don't fix it," and nowhere in military aviation does this apply more than to the C-130. This versatile cargo carrier has four Allison turboprop engines that drive it to 386 mph, but best of all they will take a 72,000-lb. airplane and allow it to fly almost 100,000 extra pounds 2,487 miles away. This is astounding, and much needed when combat operations have to happen outside the broadcast range of MTV. With modest take off and landing runway needs, and the ability to fly in almost anywhere, the C-130 is going to be around for a good long while. There's even a gun platform version (the AC-130H) that can hose down the enemy with Gatling guns and a 105mm howitzer, and this critter, known as "Spooky" or "Puff the Magic Dragon," has become the best friend of Special Forces operating on the ground.

And if you can believe it, the B-52 of Vietnam fame is still out there soldiering along, and will be for many years. There's just no better bomber ever likely to be designed. It's first flight was in April of 1952, and its eight turbojets speed of 595 mph make it the ideal long-range bomb platform, because it can carry 300,000 pounds of trouble for 10,000 miles. One hundred sixty feet long and 185 feet wide, the B-52 stands 40 feet high and needs 10,000 feet of runway to get its ponderous bulk into the sky. When Strategic Air Command needed a heavy bomber, the B-52 was the right answer, and is right up to the present day. It has a remote control rear-gun pod of either four .50-caliber machine guns or a 20mm cannon, but mostly the B-52 is expect-

The AC-130 Gunship is a stable platform that can tear up the ground in very controlled ways—always in a left-hand turn. They started this concept in Vietnam, and today have refined it so that "Puff" or "Spooky" can fire "danger close" to friendlies on the ground, and use their massive firepower to overcome a long list of targets. Besides Gatling guns and machine guns, there's even a 105mm howitzer mounted aboard these planes—an extraordinary idea of how to arm an aircraft.

The B-52 has given the U.S. fifty years of stellar service, and doesn't look to be going away any time soon. It can simply carry such a large payload such a long way that there is nothing else in our hangars that does that job as well as the B-52. The vast majority of its pilots are younger than the planes they are flying.

ed to cruise at 46,000 feet and rain hell down on earth. With many of its pilots being younger than the plane they're flying, one has to wonder what form the next heavy bomber will take—perhaps the B2-A in a larger version is slated for that task.

But another contender would be the B-1B bomber, which is a massive aircraft driven by four GE F101/102 augmented turbofans with an astounding 120,000 pounds of combined thrust. The B-1B is 147 feet long, and has swept wings that can extend to 136 feet, or retract to 78 when more maneuverability is indicated. It can blaze through the sky at 1,000 mph (about Mach 1.5) for seven thousand miles, and carry over 300,000 pounds of bombs and missiles. The B-1B also has a radar signature that is 1/100th that of the B-52. Its nose has Westinghouse APG-66 forward-looking and terrain-following radar, letting it fly as low as 300 feet off

the deck and jink through hostile valleys and past most antiaircraft systems like a gray ghost.

At the low end of the spectrum, we have the modest
Forward Air Controller (FAC). This job used to be done in World
War II by such legendary light planes as the J3 Piper Cub, which
has a four-cylinder 65hp Continental engine, and is fabric covered over metal tubing, with bungee cords for a shock absorber
system on the main landing gear. In Vietnam the plane of choice
for the FAC was a little Cessna, and there among the steaming
jungles the FACs did some amazing work as they juggled about
six radios and not only talked with ground forces, but most

*The B-1B is a massive long-distance strategic bomber with a gigantic pay-
load and staggering speeds. Although they are expensive, the B-1B is one
of America's workhorses when it comes time to fly overseas and bomb people and places with uncanny precision.*

importantly coordinated artillery and air strikes in support of the infantry. Using white phosphorus marking rockets, the FAC would orbit above the trouble and get "fast movers" (jets) to drop their ordinance "danger close" as Special Forces and others fought it out on the ground, until the problem was solved or the jets were at "Bingo Winchester" (meaning "I have just enough fuel to get home, and no more bombs or rockets").

Today's FAC has all the same daring and skill of his Vietnam predecessors, but he flies a Rockwell OV-10 Bronco. It has two 715 hp turboprops, can do 281 mph, and has a twin tail. The cockpit has excellent visibility (which is desirable if you're vectoring in jets that do 1,000 mph), and the Bronco can carry not only bombs and missiles, but also has its own three-barrel Gatling-type gun in 20mm. It can take off and land in a mere 740 feet, making it ideal for remote combat airstrips, and can also carry five paratroopers or two stretchers in a strange pod at the rear of the fuselage. Although it is being replaced by the faster OV-37, the spirit and verve of the best FACs will stay unchanged. Like the Warthog drivers, it is their job to fly low and slow and help out the troops, and at this they excel.

CHAPTER 8

Thunder on the High Seas: Modern Naval Weapons

THE U.S. NAVY is special; just ask them. With hundreds of ships, thousands of men and women, and more boats, jets, torpedoes, missiles, and guns than you can shake an anchor at, this revered service continues to provide the same security as they have throughout their long and illustrious history: control of the seas. The old saw was "If you rule the waves, you can waive the rules," but a modern updating of that might be "If you rule the waves, you can make the rules." Just as true now as it ever was, from the ancient Greeks at Salamis through the tussles of the British Empire with the Dutch, Spanish, and French fleets, right up to today's headlines, the art of waging war in an aquatic environment takes a simple idea and makes it endlessly complex, but always with the same objective in mind: dominate the ocean.

Modern sailors contemplate the battleship USS Missouri *at Pearl Harbor. These massive "battle wagons" have seen their day come and go, and their 16-inch guns are mostly replaced with missiles these days. The "dreadnaught" battles they were designed to win haven't come up much in the past fifty years, making them expensive and unwieldy members of a task force.*

With 80 percent of the globe covered by water, it should not be too surprising that mankind has spent a lot of time out on that water, as well as over and under it. All of that experience has led to a few conclusions: 1) ocean operations are extremely hazardous, even if nobody is trying to shoot and sink you, and 2) in order to pursue any kind of global control over commercial and military matters, you must have a navy that is professional to a fault, and they must practice constantly to remain that way. Just the very act of casting off the lines from a nice pier and heading out into the channel leading to the deep waters is fraught with danger—remember the battleship USS *Missouri* running aground in Chesapeake Bay, and having to be towed off by U.S. Army tugs! Popular scuttlebutt has it that the captain's last words before the mishap, having been warned by a junior officer that he was standing into danger, were: "Somebody go below and straighten out the navigator."

Simple logistics make ocean shipping the cheapest and best way to move things around the planet Earth, and that includes shoddy sneakers from Thailand, as well as cars from Japan and South Korea, and that foul-smelling stuff from the Middle East that makes those cars go. If you want to watch your choices in life reduce themselves by a power of ten, then simply cede the control of crucial choke points and the high seas to an enemy who will not allow you to move your vessels through his waters. But diplomacy has its limits, and when push comes to shove you will want to insist on the free passage of shipping— and you'll probably have to do so with a massive navy that is heavily equipped and ready to sink anything that gets in its way.

The British Navy was the paragon of excellence for many centuries (and still are, to themselves), but it was the daring and bold seamen and captains of the upstart United States who came to have the most experience and success with fighting in every part of the globe, from the North to the South Pole, and a selection of sleepy atolls, not to mention a number of beaches that are honored in memory, such as North Africa, Sicily, Anzio, Salerno, Normandy, Tarawa, Iwo Jima, and Okinawa.

A popular parlor game among a certain set is "Where

and when was the U.S. Navy founded?" There are strong cases for Marblehead, Massachusetts; Machias, Maine; Newport, Rhode Island; and even Whitehall, New York, where the restless Benedict Arnold constructed his own fleet and bashed the British on Lake Champlain during the American Revolution—this after his ill-considered but daring canoe and bateau thrust through northern Maine trying to conquer Quebec. But basically the Americans were a sea-going people, and when they were angry with their British overlords they used their nautical skills for everything from raiding Great Britain itself, to using Marblehead mariners to escape from Long Island and cross the Delaware, to attacking the best ships the Brits could muster, and more often than not knocking them silly. The United States has always been fortunate to have daring mariners who knew how to fight, such as John Paul Jones, as well as educated and influential thinkers, such a Alfred Mahan, who have kept the sea services at the forefront of national defense thinking. We have seemingly always known how to work with the ocean, be it getting to China on clipper ships with no charts, or mounting any darn gun we could find on any old garbage scow, calling it the "USS Something," and then out-maneuvering and out-fighting every other ship we came across.

Early naval weapons included cannons of varying calibers, backed up by flintlock rifles and pistols, as well as the trusty naval cutlass and the always-useful belaying pin. Sailing ships would try to position themselves so as to rake an opponent with a broadside, and then close with the enemy and board them if they weren't blown apart and sinking after the artillery portion of the disagreement. For this we needed a captain who was a master mariner as well as a swift tactician, and the Americans have always seemed to have a stock of such leaders. Cannons were not particularly accurate, but they were deadly within their limitations, and there was even clever shot with two balls con-nected by a bar or chain to wreck the enemy's rigging in its flight. Both the Revolution and the War of 1812 (and the bizarre quasi-war with France in the late eighteenth century) showed the world a force that was clever and brave, and could beat the tar out of almost anyone, including Jolly Jack Tar of the Royal Navy. We were the masters of dealing with the varying states of the ocean, as well as such arcane tactics as figuring out when to fire a broadside so that the ocean swell would position the cannon at the right angle.

The American Civil War saw the advent of ironclads, which proved very adept at trashing the wooden sailing ships they came against, and such innovations as the mortar barges used on the Mississippi (an idea revived in Vietnam). There were also more mines than previously, called confusingly "torpedoes," and even little kamikaze launches such as the one used by Lieutenant Cushing to attack a Confederate ship with a spar-tor-pedo thrust out the bows—here's a mission you don't want to volunteer for! It's a pity the captain of the USS *Cole* wasn't famil-iar with the ideas of Lieutenant Cushing …

But with President Theodore Roosevelt's "Great White Fleet" of the early 1900s we start to see a U.S. Navy that looks quite a bit like a modern fleet, and is used in some of the same ways, such as cruising around the world and pulling into harbors for "good will" visits—with the implied message: "You want a piece of me? Huh?" Guns had crept up to twelve, fourteen, and then sixteen inches, a massive weapon to mount on any platform, including a ship. There were also quick-firing guns for close-in work, and torpedoes as we know them (underwater explosive missiles), and eventually antiaircraft guns to deal with that pesky new menace, the airplane. By the time World War II engulfed the planet, naval weapons and indeed the U.S. naval service had

A lazy day during the Civil War on board the ironclad USS Monitor, *with sun protection rigged and straw hats okay for the officers. Note the revolving turret with metal screens to protect the gunners when they are loading the cannon, and the nearness to the ocean of the deck. Never the most seaworthy craft, many ironclads—including this one—went down in heavy seas.*

grown to the point where they had one of the best and earliest military intelligence departments (ONI, the Office of Naval Intelligence), battleships of a size and ferocity to scare off almost anyone, aircraft carriers and the planes needed to dominate vast patches of ocean, landing craft to set their Marine Corps ashore, submarines to sink enemy shipping, and the clout and leadership to be a major factor in winning that war. The U.S. Army had to march to Berlin, and an air-dropped atomic bomb ended things in the Pacific, but at each step of the way it was the U.S. Navy that made sure those soldiers and bombs got to where they were going, and they did so with the consummate professionalism and dry humor that has come to typify "the Navy way," as in the phrase: "There's the right way, and the wrong way, but we do things the Navy way." This includes their own private language, in which a floor is a deck, a ceiling is an overhead, a wall is a bulkhead, the bathroom is the head, and when you want to acknowledge an order you say "Aye aye!" The other services may grumble about the Navy and its budget, but they have to admit they have good food and they do an excellent job, and what more do you really want from a branch of the armed forces?

Today's Navy, having learned its lessons thoroughly by massive and concerted study through the years, operates hundreds of ships all over the world, as well as being able to project power in a variety of ways, from F-14 and F-16 jets to Navy SEAL boarding teams, who can also fight as far inland as you wish them to go. The Navy can also launch thousands of cruise missiles, protect itself from any attack from the air or sea, as well as provide safety and logistical support to any sort of conflict that is anywhere in its reach—and today that reach is global. And at sea, the same as it ever was, the captain has godlike powers that dwarf other commanders, with the one proviso: "Make sure you are right, and then go ahead." Remember the USS *Missouri*, though!

Ships

Let's start as a benchmark with the oldest commissioned ship in the U.S. Navy, the three-masted frigate USS *Constitution*, berthed

Responding to the threat of recreational boaters, the famous "Old Ironsides," the USS Constitution, fires a salvo to starboard off Boston. The sails don't seem to be pulling her along much, but some of the wonder of naval warfare in the age of "Iron Men and Wooden Ships" can be gleaned from this shot. And just imagine going all the way aloft to change sails at the captain's whim on a dark and blustery night.

at the Old Charlestown Navy Yard in Massachusetts. She's 204 feet long, has a main mast 220 feet tall, displaces 2,200 tons, and could make upward of thirteen knots with every sail deployed and running downhill. She cost $302,000 in dollars that were worth something and backed with gold when she slipped down the ways on October 21, 1797, with thirty-two 24-pounder cannons, and twenty 32-pounders. Originally built as one of six frigates to combat the Barbary Pirates (the al-Qaeda of their day), the USS *Constitution* was so massively built (including bracing her with the knees of live oak trees from Georgia) that enemy cannon balls bounced off her sides, prompting the affectionate nickname *"Old Ironsides."* Note the themes that are carried over to this day: smartly and heavily built, armed enough to defeat any similar vessel, and fast enough to run from any heavier opponent. Now you just need swabbies to man the lines and guns, and swarm onto enemy ships, junior officers of pluck and resolve, a good cook, and wise old captains who know when to fight and when to run, including when to "kedge"—the term meaning to send a longboat out ahead to drop an anchor, which is then reeled in, pulling the ship forward. This method was used in dire emergency when there was no wind, and is still valid if you lose your power plant and are drifting into danger such as a lee shore (where the wind is forcing you aground).

For comparison, let's next consider the USS *Enterprise*, which could fit five USS *Constitution*s within her length of 1,101 feet, and has a speed of 33 knots (which are nautical miles per hour). Instead of the four hundred men who crewed *Old Ironsides*, there are 3,350 men and women on the *Enterprise*. Often likened to a small city, with its own newspaper and television station, the modern aircraft carrier costs four billion or so dollars to build, but what you get for your tax dollar is a secure airfield that can go to sea and fight anywhere, which is implied by the fact that the range of the *Enterprise* is listed as "unlimited." When she rolled off the ways in 1960, she was the first nuclear-powered aircraft carrier in the world, and the most potent ship for global warfare ever devised. This is mostly due to the F-14 and F-18 jets she carries (twenty of each), as well as the twenty patrol planes and eight helicopters.

The aircraft carrier USS Enterprise *throws it into neutral after a hard turn to port. An AWACS plane can be seen on the flight deck, as well as a Phalanx Gatling up by the bridge.*

Ever since the battle of Midway (and the stalking of the German battleship *Bismarck* by torpedo planes), air power has become the essential feature of sea power, and for this reason the United States deploys as many carriers as it can, up to fifteen, in battle groups, as carriers are in essence the biggest target on the seven seas. They do have the Phalanx rapid-firing Gatling gun for close-in defense, and SAMs for antiaircraft, but other than that a carrier is a big cloud waiting to happen because the main cargo is fuel, airplanes, bombs, missiles, and rockets. It's almost as if something has to be explosive before it can go up the gangplank! For this reason they always operate with a screen of destroyers and frigates and cruisers, as well as submarines out in front and airplanes overhead, all with the same mission: "Keep the carrier safe."

But this tremendous gamble gets you a high return: the ability to control the skies anywhere there is water (and hundreds of miles inland), and a way to dominate the sea and sky in every quarter of the globe.

Next are the battleships, upgraded with Tomahawk missiles, but the days of these bad boys are numbered. There simply aren't enough enemy fleets to justify having such a huge and slow gun platform, as sad as that is for old Navy men. This class seems destined to be berthed in honored places around the country as a reminder of what really badass ships used to look like. Their 16-inch guns are not that accurate, and their day has come and gone with the sinking of the Japanese fleet.

The modern version of them is the guided missile cruiser, all 566 feet, which can do thirty knots and spew out an amazing number of Harpoon antiship missiles, as well as SAMs. Ships like the USS *Lake Erie* have two 127mm guns, two 25mm, and the ubiquitous Phalanx, although the drop in popularity of the French Exocet means that nobody has yet tried one of these in combat con-

The USS Lake Erie *is shown here launching a Standard Missile-3 (SM-3), which is an air-defense, antiballistic missile weapon. Here the flames and smoke of engine start are vented as the missile creeps up out of its launching well. Soon it will gain incredible speed and attack a target over the horizon.*

This is the guided missile destroyer USS Arleigh Burke, *named for the legendary WWII destroyer commander, who evidently never went anywhere at half speed. Modern tugs with ancient bumpers are shown horsing her into the pier, where the lines party awaits to tie her up. The white lozenge amidship is a Phalanx 20mm cannon protecting the bridge against sea-skimming missiles.*

ditions, although the cautionary tale of the British HMS *Sheffield* during the Falklands War is still in many naval minds.

Below that are the guided missile destroyers, such as the USS *Arleigh Burke* (named for a famous destroyerman of World War II, "31 Knot" Burke—but at least one old Navy guy says "Yeah, I remember Burke—he drove around at top speed and shot off all his ammunition—not that helpful."), which are 504 feet long and displace 8,300 tons (remember the USS *Constitution*

Above: The USS Jarrett *is seen here being refueled by the USS* Peliliu. *Note the welter of communication and sensory gear on the deck of the* Jarrett, *and the lone gun turret containing the Mark 45 naval gun. The rest of the* Jarrett *is missiles and engine and fuel, with some men shoehorned aboard to run it all.*

displaced 2,200 tons). She was one of the first to be equipped with the AEGIS (Greek for "shield") system which integrates all the radar tracking functions into one unit, providing 360 degree warning and offensive capabilities out to two hundred miles. The *Arleigh Burke* has a helicopter platform on the fantail (very rear of the ship), for visitors, and can launch Tomahawks, Harpoons, SAMs, and a range of other over-the-horizon missiles—close to ninety of them without replenishment. This makes for a lot of deterrent diplomacy if that's the game, and a world of hurt if talking has ended. She also has a 127mm main gun for whacking things (relatively) close up and personal.

The guided missile frigate (where are the sails?) is a tidy 453-foot package, and vessels such as the USS *Jarrett* have all the Harpoons you could want, as well as torpedoes and a 76mm main gun. Its 40,000 horsepower plant can drive it for six thousand miles at thirty knots, and that's not to be sniffed at—it's a long way from Norfolk, Virginia, to the Persian Gulf, after all. Her 323-person crew has a lot to do to keep her going, and like all destroyers and frigates, she is relatively narrow, meaning that she rolls in a heavy sea. This can range from annoying to a complete nightmare, with all the crockery in the galley (kitchen) broken, and the decks awash all the time. But this does not affect her ability to travel quickly and hit hard when she arrives, and that is in keeping with John Paul Jones saying he wished to have a fast ship, because he intended to go "in harm's way."

The amphibious assault ship USS Boxer *starts a turn to port. Notice that it's always a nice day in official photographs—no wind, no waves. The actual experience of oceanic cruising may be different. All those helicopters can transport a passel of Marines ashore in jig time, and swift craft can also deploy out of the stern well.*

The aircraft carrier USS Nimitz *is shown here sidling up to the USS* Bridge *for a VERTREP (vertical replenishment). All that stuff on the* Bridge's *stern is about to come across to the* Nimitz, *and should be enough to keep ten sailors supplied for ten minutes. Cruising in close proximity like this gives the helmsman a fit, but is a time honored way to get stuff aboard at sea. It gets even more exciting in heavy weather.*

But what if you have to get ashore and speak personally with angry locals? For that you'll want the USS *Boxer*, the largest amphibious landing ship in the world at 844 feet, a combination Harrier jump-jet platform and landing ship that can also carry two thousand U.S. Marines, which is enough to settle most disputes. You can launch and land helicopters on the deck topside, or open the massive doors to allow the landing craft (including the amazing LCACs, the air-cushion monsters of that class of vessel—"No beach out of reach" as they say) to disgorge their USMC teeth and fangs on their way to a hostile beach.

Fast combat support ships? Well, that sounds better than slow combat support, doesn't it? Ships like the USS *Bridge* are used for this, and if her lines don't inspire you to write knock-offs of Masefield ("I must go down to the sea again, to the lonely sea and sky/and all I ask is a tall ship, and a star to sail her by"), this is offset by her ability to move a 754-foot vessel at twenty-five knots for six thousand miles, displacing a staggering 48,500 tons. Wow. The *Bridge* can give other ships fuel and ammunition while underway, and even carries replacement jet engines (where do you stow that on a Boston whaler?). This compares with the relatively petite USNS *Kilauea*, which is a mere 564 feet long and has a paltry displacement of 20,169 tons. She's strictly an ammunition ship, and as such, if you're not looking for more fuel or ammo (or jet engines in crates), you'll want to cruise well away from these highly combustible craft. But when you need them, nothing else will do. Oddly, the *Kilauea* has no armament other than two helicopters—to flee the ship if threatened? But that's not the Navy way...

The USNS *Niagara Falls* is a combat stores ship of 581 feet that displaces 17,381 tons, and can cruise at twenty knots. Her 176-person crew is responsible for everything that isn't fuel or bombs, missiles, and rockets, and you'd be staggered at how much stuff it takes to keep all these ships at sea for months on end, everything from toilet paper to sextants, and each item, of course, has an incomprehensible naval code so you can have entire conversations consisting of nothing but numbers and letters. There are also fleet oilers like the USS *Platte* for when the needle on your vessel is at "E," and given the size of the world's oceans, that's most of the time.

Any of these can be brought to Davy Jones' locker (traditional term for the bottom of the sea) by a range of hazards, including small fast craft with suicidal fanatics (as in the case of the USS *Cole*, although she remained afloat due to an incredible job by her Damage Control Team), rogue waves, typhoons, enemy planes, missiles, guns, and torpedoes … and mines, those insidious and passive-aggressive explosive balls that lurk in every ocean, and especially in naval chokepoints like the Persian Gulf, Red Sea, and Sea of Japan. For those they need ships like the USS *Sentry*, which is a mine hunter in a cute 224-foot platform that can do all of 13.5 knots (shades of *Old Ironsides*!). But speed isn't the game here—they use the latest detection methods to find and neutralize mines anywhere in the world. You won't be surprised if I tell you that mine hunters get sunk by mines pretty often, which is part of the job and better than the USS *Enterprise* taking one on her keel.

And then there are the little fellers, including the 80-foot long Mark V SEAL Delivery Craft, and the 35-foot Rigid Inflatable Hull boat, both of which are used for projecting power where you don't have room to stuff a 1,000-foot-long aircraft carrier. Both were designed to be used to land SEAL teams, send over boarding parties, as well as to secure U.S. Navy ships in "friendly" ports like the one our "allies" run in Yemen. The Navy has never rescinded or modified the intent of the order "Prepare to repel boarders!" and the phrase has a new ring today, when

The Military Sealift Command Combat Stores ship USNS Niagara Falls *doing almost ten knots. Chances are, if you need something, it's aboard the* Niagara Falls. *If you have a lot of rank and pull, maybe that helicopter on the fantail will bring you what you need. Otherwise you'll have to use the small boat on the starboard side, or come alongside her and pass the stuff with lines.*

The USS Sentry, *a mine countermeasures ship, is shown here cruising north up the Hudson River past the Pallisades. Note the drones aft that can be streamed to find mines, and hopefully keep them away from aircraft carriers and tanker ships—even if the USS* Sentry *has to take one for the team.*

The Los Angeles-class sub USS **Greenville** cruises on the surface, showing the new Advanced SEAL Delivery System (ASDS) perched aft of the conning tower. This is a 65-foot minisub that has two crew members and can carry eight SEALs to shore dry-shod and happy.

those boarders wish to ram a high-speed motorboat full of explosives into the side of your nice ship. They don't actually want to come aboard—they just want to kill you (and themselves) and sink your ship.

Lurking in the depths of the ocean like massive steel whales are the submarines, including the fifty-one Los Angeles-class nuclear boats (the only U.S. Navy ship to be called a boat is the sub), which is as long as a cruiser and twice as deadly, as they can slip all but undetected through the sea and launch both nuclear and tactical missiles. The British Royal Navy rejected the first subs offered to them because they deemed the very concept to be "ungentlemanly," and they were right, but as the German, Japanese, Russian, and British subs proved, not to mention the stalwart U.S. Navy submariners, the idea is a great one if you

This is an artist's conception of how the newly-converted tactical trident submarines will look, if they are in a fish tank. The USS Ohio, *USS* Michigan, *USS* Florida, *and USS* Georgia *will be revamped to carry 154 Tomahawk missiles, far more than their current load, and will also be able to carry unmanned drones (both aerial and aquatic) and 66 SEALs if the Tomahawks don't get the job done.*

Harkening back to the legendary U.S. naval commander, the USS John Paul Jones *has "begun to fight" in this photo. The Mark 45 5-inch, .54-caliber naval gun is shown to good effect sending out a round from its unmanned turret, as the empty shell casings are automatically ejected on the deck where swabbies will recycle them, or shovel them overboard as in the "bad old days." Note the missile hatches just aft of the gun, and the anchor winch forward by the bows.*

want to win at all costs. Nothing shuts down the enemy like the notion of these monsters launching "tin fish" (torpedoes)—just ask the Argentineans, who suspended most of their naval actions after the Royal Navy took out the battleship *Belgrano* in the Falklands War.

Guns

Naval gunnery is a topic of much debate right now, and that's just the way naval gunnery officers like it. There's no debate in the mind of the person that's nicknamed "Guns" (as naval gunners always are), but they like the fact that at least some of these missile-happy policy wonks appreciate the smell of cordite and the definitive punch that only a naval cannon can offer. "Guns" has never seen a combat situation that couldn't be improved by concentrated shelling, and at the least they always want to "fire for effect." In hardly any other sphere is a cannon as useful as it is at sea, for everything from firing warning shots across the bows of vessels when you wish to express the message implied by the single-flag signal X (known as "X-Ray," and meaning "Stop carrying out your intentions and watch for my signals"), to blasting the hell out of an enemy vessel or beach.

The standard modern U.S. Navy gun is a 5-inch (127mm) automatic cannon with a range of about sixty-three nautical miles. There are still many old-timers who swear by the 5-inch, and this modern one has both a fantastic range and accuracy, as well as being able to fire a whole candy store of munitions, from star shells to smoke to a 70-pound explosive shell that will really let the light in. This Mark 45 5-inch/54-caliber gun can spit out about twenty rounds a minute, and do so on its own without a crew in its turret.

Want more rounds per minute? You need the Mark 75 3-inch/62-caliber, which is a 76mm cannon that gets up to eighty-five rounds per minute, although the range goes down to 8.7 nautical miles. Also unmanned, there are hoppers below deck that can hold 40, 80, or 115 rounds (for when things just need a good hosing). Both the Mark 45 and Mark 75 are linked to a fire-control system that acquires targets and nails them, and gunners

The Phalanx MK-15 Close-in Weapons System blurts out a fast 500 rounds of 20mm ammunition, evidently at a target that is not only close but at forty degrees elevation. The Phalanx was a response to the Exocet missile attacks of the Falklands War, and can detect and hose down automatically any fast sea-skimming target as it approaches a vessel. It does not work on suicide boats, but against missiles the promise is that 4,500 rounds a minute through this modified Gatling gun will be enough to neutralize almost any threat.

are a little put off by that, as they like to lay their own cannons, but they like saying "Target destroyed, Sir," even better.

The all-bets-are-off gun is the Phalanx Mark 15 Close-in Weapon System, which is a big white dome with a Gatling gun sticking out one side, and a nervous temperament. You simply flip the switch, and this puppy starts scanning around, and when it sees something it doesn't like (hopefully not the admiral's gig!), it blows the crap out of it by revolving the barrels at high speed and sending out so much lead the size of 25mm shells that hardly anything could approach you any closer, even if it wished to, and that includes low-flying aircraft and sea-skimming missiles. At an alarming rate of 4,500 rounds per minute, and with a range of about 2,000 yards (maximum), the Phalanx has yet to be tried, but it's hard not to like the concept, especially if you're the nervous type. What enemy threat doesn't need a ten-second burst of 500 one-inch shells?

An old Navy officer used to say when teaching navigation: "Someday they'll have a machine that gives you your location, course and speed, and spits out a Hershey bar." Well, except for the chocolate, we have those machines and a lot more today. Modern naval warfare is among the most complex and dangerous of all military operations, and it is a tribute to the men and women of the U.S. Navy that it has been studied and honed to a place where there isn't a navy in the world that can even come close to messing with us. Our computers and weapons are second to none, and our supply and variety of ships is larger than any four other navies put together. With the fall of the Soviet Union, and the unfortunate history of the Chinese navy, it seems likely that the United States will be able to dominate the seas for the next fifty years at least. But knock off the gloating, and belay any talk about letting down our guard, because none of this great weaponry nor any of these massive ships is going anywhere to do anything without the brave men and women who make it all happen, from the most junior rating to the crustiest old admiral still thinking about Lieutenant Cushing and the battle of Jutland in 1916. There is a tradition of understatement in the Navy, and especially in signaling by Morse or flags, but our entire nation can thank the U.S. Navy for a good part of the success of our military operations as well as any peace and security that exists around the world, and for that we owe them the traditional brief signal given when the highest praise is implicit: "Well Done."

CHAPTER 9

Frankenstein's War: Technology

IN 1930 THE FABLED Winchester Arms Company decided to make a gun that was much more robust and well made than any that had ever come before. After an exhausting series of tests, there emerged the legendary Model 21, one of the all time classics. Winchester engineers had used a special "purple pill," a cartridge that was purposefully built to be overloaded and dangerous, and had tested a wide variety of weapons, as well as their new design, with the specific intent of making them fail. In what must have been an alarming week of eruptions and explosions, no other gun got beyond firing 305 of these "purple pills" before something really unfortunate happened, such as the barrels bursting or the action flying to pieces, while the Model 21 went through a staggering two thousand rounds with no evidence of any harm to the gun. But the Model 21 wasn't a military rifle; it was a top-break sporting shotgun with side-by-side barrels, and is still one of the strongest and most elegant weapons ever made.

In this anecdote we can see a few of the hallmarks of technology at war: engineers trying to best the competition, and wealth as a driving factor in weapons design and development. Because the Model 21 was a gentleman's gun, a great deal of time was put into it, and the cost was commensurately high. Gentlemen like things like that. Often this had been the story with firearm progress through the years, as hunters demanded something less temperamental than the old flintlock ignition system, for instance, and so the percussion cap made its appearance; first on the sporting fields and forests, and soon enough on the killing fields of battle. Due to impatient and hotheaded gentry, some of the first and finest percussion cap pistols were made in pairs for dueling. With the rise of industrial states the scope of battle and warfare expanded to the point where not only were there more deadly technologies applied to firearms, but great efforts were made across the board in whatever endeavor seemed to show the most promise of aiding the soldiers in the field, and winning lucrative contracts for the supply of more-or-less effective technologies to the art of slaying the foe. The young J. P. Morgan's foray into arms dealing comes to mind, where he not only sold defective uniforms to the Union (known as "shoddy" for good reason), but also managed to turn a great deal on muskets with only one or two problems, such as exploding upon firing and taking off the fingers or hand of the unlucky end user. He had bought them in a lot marked "unfit for service" and managed to turn them around for a good profit. After all, the fate of the nation might be at stake and many average young men might be dying on battlefields from Texas to Pennsylvania, but for well-connected young "go ahead" men like Mr. Morgan it was pretty simple to pay $300 to avoid the draft and then get down to the serious business of cutting deals. Not that any of our modern arms companies would ever do such a thing.

Trevor Dupuy has an absorbing chart in one of his books showing the relative rise of various weapons systems, and he seems to estimate that the average chap using a sword, spear, or axe can dispatch twenty men in one hour. Needless to say, the chart spikes like the North Wall of the Eiger when it gets to machine guns and nuclear bombs.

Interestingly, however, the simple rate of killing isn't the benchmark of an effective weapon, and technology alone has not proved to be the most important factor in winning wars, despite our deep-seated and bloody-minded admiration for more efficient butchering. As one general has observed, "If technology alone were the deciding factor, the Vietnam War would have been over in about six weeks." Be that as it may, we have seen the emergence of more gadgets and doodads in the past century than at any other time in history, and not a few of them have either their roots or their subsequent career firmly in the field of military operations.

The modern American soldier is draped and festooned with a long list of high-tech devices, and it is one of the jarring factors of modern war that along with traditional red and blue arrows sweeping across the map (in places like Tikrit and Baghdad, for instance), there is an entire phantom world of technology wrapped like an invisible cocoon around any modern military action. So let's start with an average 22-year-old corporal from Buffalo, New York, who is on outpost duty in a mythical hostile landscape. He's had a long night of it, fighting off sleep, and trying not to get freaked out by himself in the dark at his Observation Post (OP). But fortunately he has night-vision goggles (Generation III, which work in total darkness), and a bionic ear (a very sensitive microphone aimed at the expected source of

trouble), and Claymore mines rigged up to both trip wires as well as triggers he can activate himself, and a night-vision scope on his M4 carbine, and MREs (Meals Ready to Eat) for when he gets peckish, and a hydration tube to suckle upon, and a radio for chatting up his sergeant, who oddly has no taste for small talk. Suddenly there is movement and noise to the front. This is it. A shape appears in the distance, and in a moment the entire military machine is set in motion, with headquarters being alerted as our corporal prepares to fight for his life. Word goes out to heavy machine guns and tube-launched, shoulder-fired and vehicle mounted missiles on the flanks, to batteries of artillery to the rear, as well as tanks and fighting vehicles ready to pounce, and far out at sea the F-14s and F-18s are warming up on the deck of an aircraft carrier. The GPS coordinates have been downloaded and uplinked so that any one of a bewildering variety of bombs, rockets, and missiles can be vectored onto the exact spot where the threat is looming. Hands are poised over the launching trigger that will unleash Tomahawk missiles from ships and trucks, and ears are peeled for the updated "sitrep" ("Situation Report") coming in through scrambled satellite phones. High overhead those same satellites are sending real-time images of the action on the ground, both to the commander on the scene as well as back to the boys at the Pentagon (and some curious chaps at Fort Meade, Maryland, as well as their buddies in Langley, Virginia) and even to the White House.

A young U.S. Marine ready to "own the night." He is wearing an AN/PVS-7B NVG (and don't screw those letters and numbers up on the requisition form, OK?), which will allow him to pierce the darkness and engage in combat well past "lights out." And don't worry—his sergeant will tell him to put a clip in his M16 before the shooting starts.

Our corporal has begun to sweat, but he is wearing polypro garments and Gore-Tex which allow him to perspire without getting chilled (what they wouldn't have given to have this at the siege of Sebastopol!). His bulletproof Kevlar vest is a comfort, as are the grenades he has stacked near to hand, and his Nomex fireproof gloves. In his new digital camouflage he is pretty sure that he is blending into the landscape well enough to give him the first shot, and his infrared sensors are allowing him to see through the darkness, smoke, mist, and driving rain which seem to be an obligation of combat at night. Back stateside, the president has been woken up (with a report of the poll numbers in California, as well as an item detailing the corporal's sounding of the alarm), and generals and colonels have clustered together in the War Room to ponder this threat. Could this be the big one? They scan the full range of incoming data, which also shows that the Chinese have touched off a space shot at their lovely and remote Base 20, and the North Koreans are massing in their tunnels for no known good reason, and a shipment of missiles has just been intercepted off the coast of Yemen, tracked by satellites and originally brought to light by an agent aboard the ship, and in Colombia the FARQ has shifted one valley closer to Bogotá. No, there's no pattern, they think, and so they focus on the corporal in his hole waiting for the unknown, as well as the images coming in from the UAVs (unmanned aerial vehicles, such as the Predator). As the menacing shape grows clearer in his night-vision goggles, it gives off a petrifying bellow, and they can all stand down. It's a wild camel, bent on finding a lady camel, and not an enemy sapper looking to throw satchel charges around and slit the throat of unsuspecting young men on lookout duty. Lest the reader think that mere whimsy drives this illustration, keep in mind that several camels were slain in similar circumstances in Afghanistan, and that the doomed dromedaries were most in danger at night. Can you claim that your nerves would not be a trace on edge pulling such duty? Or that you wouldn't "spray and pray" with whatever weapon came to hand?

But notice how the technology permeates the action, in every phase from the initial warning to the "all clear," and also how the one piece of gear that remains squirrelly and erratic is the person himself. Technology has failed to give us steady nerves for some reason. And notice that just as with fire or the wheel, you have to keep an eye on the gear to make sure you're not streaming flames as you roll along. Old ideas are recombined with the latest laboratory breakthroughs, and sometimes the results are astounding. Just keep in mind the dangers and fail-ures that come with any piece of gear. Pilots have a saying that the cute little flashlights they keep in their flight bags are simply a device for storing dead batteries.

Nowlet's kick open the doors of the U.S. arsenal and take a brief look at some of the strange and wonderful weapons that we have been deploying just recently during the past several sea-sons of warfare, shall we? No loose hair or neckties please, don't choke on the acronyms, and don't touch anything as we pass through, all right?

Our sensors have gotten better and better with each passing war, so that the fine field glasses and radar of World War II are all but outmoded. We can use laser designators (some in very small packages) to "light up" a target, and then the new generation of "smart bombs" can ride the beam right down and onto the target. Most of us got our first look at this during the 1991 Gulf War, when part of the daily briefing was the very best nose camera footage of targets being destroyed with an ease and precision that would have floored Billy Mitchell. And we're talk-ing about third generation infrared as well, in weapons like the JDAMs (Joint Direct Attack Munitions), which can be launched

This Navy F/A-18C Hornet has just pickled off a Joint Direct Attack Munitions (JDAMS), which is a GPS equipped 1,000- or 2,000-lb. smart bomb that can find its way to anywhere on the battlefield with a precision that enemies find most unwelcome.

by everything from the B1 bomber to helicopters, and unerringly (almost) find their way to the enemy's position. But we can drop many other types of munitions as well, including good old-fashioned napalm (which is basically gasoline and detergent to make it a flammable foam that sticks to things and burns for a long time) to thermobaric bombs that not only have a huge fireball, but also send a pressure wave ahead of their explosions that bodes ill for cave dwellers and maddened clerics. And these come in a variety of styles, from the USMC's shoulder-launched multipurpose assault weapon (SMAW), which has a fireball and a concussive blast, as well as the ability to turn corners in flight

The modern bazooka, the SMAW (Shoulder-fired Multi-purpose Assault Weapon), is seen here on the right. Large enough to tackle many light tanks if you shoot at the weak points (treads, viewing ports, joint between the turret and the hull), the SMAW was also used in Afghanistan to probe the entrances to caves.

and even go upstairs, to the USAF's BLU-118/B, which is a laser-guided bunker buster that first penetrates the ground to quite a good depth, and then goes off with the familiar fireball and concussion. But what if we're attacking a suspected ammo dump containing chemical and biological weapons? The last thing we want is to blow them all over the battlefield, endangering our own troops as well as any civilians and camels in the general facility. Well, for that we'll need the high-temperature incendiary (HTI) weapon, which burns at 1,000 degrees Fahrenheit for quite a good long time, and hopefully consumes whatever noxious materials have been found.

Cluster bombs, meaning one container with several "bomblets" inside, have had a decided vogue in the last forty years, and the CBU-97 Sensor Fused Weapon (SFW) is a good example. Weighing in at a half ton, this puppy has ten BLU-108s inside four smart Skeet warheads, making for forty bomblets that can cover an area of up to thirty acres, and each one can be made to home in on an armored vehicle or other designated target. For designation, often U.S. Special Forces are the main man, using handheld laser designators to "paint" likely looking places, people, vehicles, and structures. They are also hooked into the Predator drone through a software system known as "Rover," and this enables them to not only see real-time images, but also to transmit those images to any number of end users, from the AC-130 gunship circling overhead (always to the left, as that is where the gun mounts are), to the AH-64D Apache Longbow, which has a fire-control radar that can detect and classify up to 128 separate targets, and pick the sixteen most imminently dangerous ones for an immediate hammering by either its own 30mm chain gun, or the new Hydra rockets, or the venerable and accurate radar-guided AGM-114 Hellfire missile.

The use of drones and robots in the field is one of the

What happens when you cross a remote-control ATV with the USMC? You get the Gladiator. The Gladiator is designed to give a remote capability to Marines on the ground, and to sneak into places where it would be dangerous to send a person. It has day and night cameras, chemical detectors, can generate smoke, and you can mount everything from a SAW to the M240G medium machine gun, or an Uzi. It can also breach obstacles and minefields. The controls were designed for young military men who are experienced with computer games.

Once the realm of old men and geeky kids, the remote-controlled aerial vehicle has surged to the front with the deployment of the Predator, which can transmit real-time infrared and color video back to intelligence analysts and commanders sitting safely in the control vehicle. The laughter at its pusher propeller and strange design stopped when a Predator was used in Yemen to disrupt (fatally) a motoring tour by al-Qaeda operatives. The CIA had managed to graft Hellfire missiles onboard, and when they confirmed the identities of the car's occupants, that was all she wrote.

fastest growing aspects of modern technology at war, and evidently very small PackBots have been used in Afghanistan and Iraq, including the shadowy "Dragon Eyes," which seems to be a small flying sensor drone that can be carried into the field and deployed right out of the Alice pack. The Israelis have been using something like this for a few years to supervise their own troubles, and we seem to have caught up on the battlefield, although the full reports are not in just yet. And the notion of robots has been expanded to a number of fields. Some of the first were used in bomb disposal, including the clever small British device that rolls on little treads and has a camera and microphone as well as a 12-gauge shotgun (not the Winchester Model 21) mounted to blow holes in car windows and hopefully set off the blast while the soft and frangible humans are hunkered down at a safe remove from the blast.

Perhaps the most famous of the modern drones is the RQ-1 Predator, which is a small remotely piloted unmanned aerial vehicle (UAV). If our enemies weren't reading *Newsweek*, the light must have begun to dawn on November 3, 2002, when a Predator operated by the CIA launched two AGM-114 Hellfire missiles down onto a car in Yemen which contained (we think) some bad al-Qaeda types. All that was left was some smoking rubble and body parts. We had been watching them, and at a time and place of our choosing (perhaps when they were passing on a blind corner and exceeding the speed limit?) we blew them to paradise with very little effort.

The Predator has been in development for quite some time, including an intensive period during 1994 and 1995, at which time it was deployed to Bosnia and did fine service as it found its way in the air and sent back data of vital importance to commanders on the scene as well as policy wonks back in the Land of the Big PX. The Predator has a 26,000-foot ceiling, and can fly for five hundred miles and stay aloft for forty hours. It does all this with a Rotax Model 912 engine (curiously, also the choice of many ultralight aircraft designers) burning 100 Octane AvGas, and the four-cylinder engine drives it along at about seventy to ninety knots. At twenty-seven feet long and seven feet high, you'd hardly notice this thing above you. It stalls at fifty-four, and needs five thousand feet of runway to get aloft. There's a pilot and a payload operator safely back on the ground, and they can communicate with their flying platform by either line of site or using satellites and GPS. And what can you put aboard it? Well, obviously some pretty serious missiles. But it comes from the factory with an electro-optical/infrared (EO/IR) Versatron Skyball Model 18 sensor system, along with television broadcast abilities using both zoom and spotter lenses, and the ever-popular Westinghouse 783R234 synthetic aperture radar (SAR). It cost a mere $40 million in 1997, but who is to say what the MSRP is today?

But are we putting the cart before the horse here? How exactly do they know which stretch of unhappy desert or mountain to fly their little white drone over? For that they'll want to take a gander at the product streaming in from the satellites, such as the KH-11, which can see things down to six inches (in case we attack Lilliput?). But the problem with the KH-11 was that they were in orbit, and we only had six or seven of them in the first Gulf War, meaning that we only got shots every two or three hours. What an improvement the Advanced KH-11 Imaging Spacecraft was! It could be maneuvered from the ground, and so made it all but impossible for the enemy to know when one might be overhead. And to improve on that, we can cross correlate optical images from our KH-11s with the synthetic aperture radar (SAR—remember?) on the Lacrosse satellite, which creates high-resolution radar images. Our DSPS (Defense Support Program Spacecraft—do try to keep up, won't you?) provide infrared images of super high quality, allowing us to not only see the plumes from Scud missile launches and the afterburners on jets, but also, due to their geosynchronous orbit (meaning it orbits at the same pace as the rotation of the earth, making it hang in one spot above an area we want to know more about), an almost constant all-weather oversight of the modern battlefield. Improved Crystal is not a better lemonade, but instead the KH-12 satellite which has the ability to see invisible, near-infrared, and thermal-infrared bands, and can thus compare the heat of the ground with various structures under the ground, like bunkers and caves, and can see things as small as two and a half inches. And the KH-13 has a Stealth capability that allows it to float there undetected by enemy radar or infrared. The 8X is among the most recent satellite launches. It has an elliptical orbit and an adjustable dwell rate. With all of this hardware (or space junk depending on your point of view) drifting around obscuring the skies, it has been estimated that every part of the earth can be scanned every fifteen minutes, making skinny dipping, even at the North Pole, even less attractive than before.

But we can also operate all manner of sensing craft at much lower altitudes than the satellites. First in line is the E-3 Sentry, known as the AWACS (airborne warning and control system—see how logical this is when you get the hang of it?). You can spot the AWACS because it is an obvious USAF four engine jet with a massive rotating dome over the aft part of the fuselage. With a range of 250 miles, and the ability to see airplanes as well as stuff on the ground, the AWACS carries air traffic controllers who make sure all the air assets don't appear in the same place at the same time, but are staggered at tactical intervals. This is an all-weather command, control, and communications airplane made by Boeing that is 145 feet long and 130 feet from wingtip to wingtip. The radar dome is thirty feet across, and sticks up eleven feet from the frame of the plane. At $123 million fully rigged up, you don't want to crash these too often. And as just part of the explanation for our $400 billion dollar defense budget, we own about thirty-five of these things.

Take the old Boeing 707 and mount a bunch of "Gee Whiz!" electronics aboard her, and then you'd have a JSTARS … but at a cost of $244 million per plane. We only have about fifteen of these. It does the same old battlefield imaging that the AWACS does, but uses its radar for ground warfare management with no flight control capabilities. In a sobering reminder of the true nature of warfare, most of the photos of the interior of these planes show what look like tired men staring fixedly at screens and dials, probably waiting for some image to download. Same old same old, what?

Naturally the U.S. Navy needs its own sensing flight platform (because the USAF won't give them the frequency to listen to the AWACS or the JSTARS?), and for that they use the E-2C Hawkeye, which has a speed of three hundred knots and a crew of five. It also has a huge radar dish grafted onto the fuselage, and with this it can provide over-the-horizon early warning to the aircraft carrier that launches it. Each carrier has two of these, and if the captain is smart he keeps one aloft most of the time while he's at sea.

All of these flying platforms, from the Predator up to the AWACS and satellites, seem to work very well … except for the fact that they won't tell you what's in an enemy's head, or what he'll do next. Drat! But there is a darker side to technology at war, and that is stuff that doesn't work so good. In 1991, the evil (and elusive) Saddam launched a Scud missile at our boys in Saudi Arabia. Suddenly, streaking to the rescue came the Patriot mis-

Ever wonder how they coordinate all those jets and missiles in a big operation? The E-3 Sentry AWACS is the answer. It's a converted civilian jetliner, with a little addition—that huge rotating pod on the top of the fuselage. AWACS can detect threats, vector in air strikes, talk to everybody (including the Pentagon and the President), and do it all at high altitudes and high speed, mostly staying above any air defense.

A Navy E-2C Hawkeye gets launched from an aircraft carrier. The Navy can't operate the huge AWACS, so it has its own version, the Hawkeye. This provides early warning for the carrier battle group, and helps with one of their main missions: "Keep the carrier safe."

sile, a state of the art surface to air defense system. It appeared to home in and strike the offensive Scud. Wonder of wonders! Not only were Raytheon (the makers) and the men and women on the ground thrilled, but also the backers of the Star Wars missile defense system said "See? See? What did we tell you?" And best of all, it was called a Patriot, reinforcing all kinds of hubris and warm feelings among certain political parties that are all too willing to wrap themselves in the flag instead of actually guarding the freedoms in the Bill of Rights. As it turns out, it would have been more efficient to throw rocks at Scuds. There is precious little evidence that the Patriot hit anything at all, and instead of that it struck pieces of the Scuds as they broke up (being manufactured with little care or ability by North Korea and other unindustrial powerhouses) and caused greater destruction on the ground than if the soldiers had simply come out of their bunkers and waved their fists at the streaking missiles overhead. Turns out there was a programming error of a rather alarming magnitude in the guidance system. One would think Raytheon would be passed over with their next bright idea, but instead of that we have the Patriot (PAC-3) surface-to-air missile system, and disturbing rumors that instead of focusing exclusively on why their system didn't work, the company was equally concerned with the PR implications of the public's perception of how the system worked. J. P. Morgan would be proud.

But then there are interesting things like the CBU-94 Blackout Bomb, and the BLU-114/B Soft Bomb. The Blackout Bomb carries submunitions that explode and send out fine strands of highly conductive carbon, which shorts out everything it touches such as wires and vehicles. As a way to disrupt the power grid without hurting anyone, the CBU-94 is pointing the way to a future of weapons that are effective even if they don't fill up an enemy's graveyards. When dropped by the F-117A Nighthawk (as in Bosnia and Baghdad), the stealth and surprise of all the power going out ought to at least equal the consternation felt in much of the northeastern United States during the summer of 2003, when the lights went out due to a tree hitting a line ... or so it was said.

This also launches us into the very spooky and dark world of new weaponry, such as the acoustic cannon. Evidently at five miles you can hear it, at a half mile you are in a fair amount of pain,

The eternal military question: "Where the Hell is THIS? I don't recall an ocean on my map!" Actually, this Navy engineer is sizing up the amphibious landing possibilities of this beach using Global Positioning Satellite data and a digital camera. This is the military issue GPS unit; some Special Forces use civilian models that are a good bit smaller, such as the Garmin eTrex.

and at one hundred yards you will void your bowels and die. As to whether this is somehow preferable, better or more humane than being shot, the jury is still out on that one. We also have lasers that can cut metal (and humans), blinding flashes of light that can render an enemy permanently qualified for that handicapped parking space, and even bombs that cause earthquakes (useful for those persnickety cave dwellers), as well as passive listening devices both under the ocean (U.S. Navy) and in the sky (NSA, NRO). It can seem at times that mankind is much more intent upon killing and spying upon one another than it is with feeding or educating the masses around the globe. Then there's the ultra miniaturized transistors and particle detectors, and, of course, our own and other's stocks of Anthrax, Sarin, and BZ gas, not to mention the remote viewing projects of the last thirty years or experiments with mind control. Everything's a weapon when you think about it the right (or wrong) way! Why, the so-called "Acoustic Kitty" is a prime example, in which our scientists rigged up a cat so that he was a recording device. Evidently the tests were aborted when the cat ran into traffic and was run over.

But before we kick closed the door on our warehouse of high-tech warfare, let's consider the lowly tools used for handwriting. NASA spent a boatload of money for a pen that could write in space, under zero gravity, upside down, underwater, in any and all conditions. The defense applications were also considered, and this thing would work at zero degrees just as well as it would at 150. It was thus with some consternation that once we began to exchange astronauts and cosmonauts with the Russians that we discovered they had also grappled with this thorny problem, and had found a solution. The Russians used a pencil.

Daunting as that may be, there can be no doubt that we are entering an age of technology when warfare will advance by leaps and bounds. And there may even be some benefits for you and me amidst all this weaponry. Firefighters and Search and Rescue personnel are already using thermal imaging to search for lost humans in both flaming houses and across cold mountain ranges, and GPS has revolutionized boating and hiking (just don't forget those spare batteries!). And the Digital Scene Matching And Correlation (DSMAC) used to get cruise missiles around hostile countries may soon be coming to your heads-up display on your windshield. What fun it will be spilling coffee on the Navstar system while stuck in traffic! And how will your insurance company deal with it when you are struck from behind by a RPV (remotely piloted vehicle)?

In Britain they call scientists "boffins," and this seems like a good term for the "Wizards of Armageddon" who labor tirelessly to exploit every facet of reality and unreality to a hostile end. From infrared (below the wavelength we can see) to ultraviolet (above), and from the depths of the ocean to the very stars above, the one thing that seems sure is that everything that can be weaponized will be. And then it will just be up to us to determine when such weapons should be used—the same as with your trusty old battle axe or Winchester Model 21, eh?

CHAPTER 10

America's Arsenal of the Future

THE ONE THING we can be sure of is that in the field of arms and warfare, there will always be new wrinkles, and new ways to skin cats and strike the enemy. This makes it more important than ever to have public discussions about new technologies, instead of just rounds of funding and massive projects working off in the weeds, such as the missile defense system now in development up in Alaska. So far the project has cost millions of dollars, and the general in charge of it has stated that they have yet to see a success in intercepting and destroying an incoming missile. In fact some experts have likened the task to trying to hit one rifle bullet with another. Good shot, if you can pull it off.

It's easy to forget the fact that there has yet to be a battlefield innovation that simply swept the field. The massive German guns that destroyed the Belgian forts at the beginning of World War I did not tip the tide for long in the Germans' favor. The flamethrower, tank, and airplane were each astounding in their debuts, but did not prove to be the war-winning devices that their inventors and deployers had predicted. But then, we have yet to see a massive nuclear, chemical, and biological offensive, or the results of one. And while it seems safe to state that the United States would never strike first with such a devastating array of horrors, we might well respond to such an attack in kind on a larger scale—if we can figure out who to hit. And, in another bit of happy biowar news, we've just come up with a mousepox virus that not only sickens the wee, slickit, timorous mousies, but also suppresses their immune systems, so that in tests every mouse infected died. Keep in mind that humans are a lot more like mice than it's comfortable to contemplate.

But it's far too easy to get carried away with nightmare scenarios. A more mundane consideration of weapons deployment is the simple matter of logistics. It has been said that amateurs discuss tactics and strategy, while the professionals are talking logistics a mile a minute. To get the bullets and beans up to the front no longer usually involves mules, but in some sort of pack animal's revenge, the ethos of the cranky mule remains firmly in place when it comes time to fill out those requisition papers and start the long chain of events to actually get a new box of ammo for a SAW.

It would seem that warfare and the institutional use of weapons is such a crap shoot, and one that hinges on so many variables, that the only sensible way to pursue it is with excellent leadership, intelligence, and planning long before any shots are fired, and then to use the very best and exactly right weapons at a furious pace so that you light the fuse, hit like a hammer, and you're done. The aircraft designer Burt Rutan says that the best way to operate is to use the lowest level technology you can for accomplishing your aims, not the highest tech. Remember the Russian pencil? Mr. Rutan could hardly be accused of being a Luddite, and you would hope that his clever and sensible ideas would be pondered at that big five-sided building on the Potomac where they issue the marching orders.

Sun Tzu, the ancient Chinese general, as well as U.S. Army Field Manual 100-5 (Fighting Future Wars), both counsel their readers that a prolonged war is to be heartily avoided. That clever and sly Sun Tzu also says that the height of excellence is not to win one hundred battles, but instead to accomplish one's goals and defeat the enemy without fighting. Contained within Sun Tzu's obviously demented blithering is the tweedy notion that empathy (not sympathy—look up the difference) is one of the most valuable tools in your bag of weapons. It rather reminds me of the way you can sometimes not get your eye lined up correctly with a telescopic sight, so that instead of the reticule and target you are expecting to see, what appears is your own large Mark One Eyeball staring back at you. Weapons have a funny way of bringing up Walt Kelly's statement (as voiced by the ineducable possum, Pogo): "We have met the enemy, and he is us."

Our current occupation of Iraq is costing us a billion dollars a week and casualties up the wazoo, and while we have caught the disheveled madman who used to run the country, we don't seem to be any closer to finding his WMDs—which is what this dance was supposed to be about. This is not because we failed to deploy enough weapons. Let's review the preceeding paragraph, shall we? War is a stern master and abrupt teacher, and it's curious to watch the finest military force in the world seemingly floundering not because of a lack of good people or the means to kill and subdue any threat on the planet, but for other very simple reasons. Did someone not get that memo about guerrilla warfare and the difficulties involved? A seemingly ad hoc lash-up of lunatics and homicidal maniacs is using very low-tech means to keep us off balance, including many of our own shoulder-launched missiles. We have a $500 buy-back program in place, but maybe we shouldn't have flooded the country with our weapons to begin with? Just a thought.

We've come quite a long way in the development of arms, and there are new technologies emerging all the time. Hopefully you've learned a few things from reading all of this, and either agreed or disagreed with some of my asides, but if it made you think a few new thoughts then I'll feel it has all been worthwhile. And while I stoutly agree with the blunt general who says that "Hope is not a method," it may well turn out that of all our means of achieving our goals, in warfare as well as in life, hope is the finest weapon of them all.

•

Bibliography

Batchelor, John and Hogg, Ian. *Artillery*. New York: Ballantine Books, 1972.

Benson, Ragnar. *David's Tool Kit: A Citizens' Guide to Taking Out Big Brother's Heavy Weapons*. Port Townsend, WA: Loompanics Unlimited, 1997.

Bonds, Ray, ed. *The Illustrated Directory of Modern American Weapons*. New York: Prentice Hall, 1986.

Bradin, James W. *From Hot Air to Hellfire: The History of Army Attack Aviation*. Novato, CA: Presidio Press, 1994.

Brodie, Bernard and Fawn. *From Crossbow to H-Bomb*. New York: Dell, 1962.

Campbell, John T. *Desert War: The New Conflict Between the U.S. and Iraq*. New York: Penguin Putnam, 2003.

Collier, Larry. *How To Fly Helicopters*. New York: McGraw-Hill, 1986.

Crawford, Steve. *Twenty-First Century Warships: Surface Combatants of Today's Navies*. St. Paul, MN: MBI Publishing, 2002.

Dunnigan, James F. *How to Make War: A Comprehensive Guide to Modern Warfare*. New York: Quill, 1983.

Dunnigan, James F. and Bay, Austin. *A Quick & Dirty Guide to War*. New York: Quill, 1991.

Fitzsimons, Bernard. *Tanks & Weapons of World War I*. New York: Beekman House, 1973.

Forty, Simon, et al. *Lock & Load: Weapons of the US Military*. New York: Sterling Publishing, 2002.

Gabriel, Richard A. *Military Incompetence: Why the American Military Doesn't Win*. New York: Hill and Wang, 1985.

Gunston, Bill. *History of Military Aviation.* New York: Sterling Publishing, 2003.

Harding, David, and Grey, Randal, eds. *Weapons: An International Encyclopedia from 5000 BC to 2000 AD.* New York: St. Martin's Press, 1990.

Hartung, William D. *And Weapons For All.* New York: HarperCollins, 1995.

Hogg, Ian V. *Machine Guns: 14th Century to Present.* Iola, WI: Krause Publications, 2002.

Hogg, Ian V., and Weeks, John S. *Military Small Arms of the 20th Century* (7th Edition). Iola, WI: Krause Publications, 2000.

Lewer, Nick and Schofield, Steven. *Non-Lethal Weapons: A Fatal Attraction?* London: Zed Books, 1997.

Lyon, Hugh. *An Illustrated Guide to Modern Warships.* London: Salamander Books, 1980.

Schnabel, Jim. *Remote Viewers: The Secret History of America's Psychic Spies.* New York: Dell, 1995.

Shukman, David. *Tomorrow's War: The Threat of High-Technology Weapons.* New York: Harcourt Brace, 1996 (uncorrected proof).

Small, Captain E. G. *Notes On Fire Control 1940.* Washington, D.C.: United States Government Printing Office, 1941.

Sullivan, Gordon R., and Harper, Michael V. *Hope is Not a Method.* New York: Broadway Books, 1996.

Sunt, Captain Wilbur A. *Naval Science 4.* Annapolis, MD: Naval Institute Press, 1990.

Waldron, Major William H. *The Infantry Soldier's Handbook (1917).* New York: The Lyons Press, 2000.

Wheeler, Barry C. *Modern American Fighters and Attack Aircraft.* New York: Prentice Hall, 1987.

Index